THE *GAME*
I'LL NEVER *FORGET*

as told to
George Vass

As originally published by

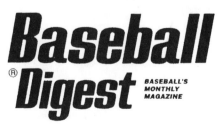

Copyright © 1999 by Bonus Books, Inc. and *Baseball Digest*

All rights reserved

Except for appropriate use in critical reviews or works of scholarship,
the reproduction or use of this work in any form or by any electronic,
mechanical or other means now known or hereafter invented, including
photocopying and recording, and in any information storage and
retrieval system is forbidden without the written permission of the
publisher.

Library of Congress Cataloguing in Publication Data

ISBN 1-56625-128-X

Cover design by Karen Sheets

Bonus Books, Inc.
160 East Illinois Street
Chicago, IL 60611

First Edition

Printed in the United States of America

THE LINEUP

1. Walter Alston
2. Luis Aparicio
3. Ernie Banks
4. Vida Blue
5. Bobby Bonds
6. Lou Boudreau
7. Orlando Cepeda
8. Ron Cey
9. Roberto Clemente
10. Tony Conigliaro
11. Roger Craig
12. Jose Cruz
13. Larry Doby
14. Moe Drabowsky
15. Don Drysdale
16. Ron Fairly
17. Tim Foli
18. Steve Garvey
19. Jim Gilliam
20. Tommy Henrich
21. Catfish Hunter
22. Jim Kaat
23. Ralph Kiner
24. Tony Kubek
25. Frank Lane
26.
27.
28. Juan Marichal
29. Billy Martin
30. Gene Mauch
31. Willie Mays
32. Tim McCarver
33. Johnny Mize
34. Lindsey Nelson
35. Al Oliver
36. Claude Passeau
37. Tony Perez
38. Lou Piniella
39. Dan Quisenberry
40. Pee Wee Reese
41. Rick Reuschel
42. Jerry Reuss
43. Brooks Robinson
44. Al Rosen
45. Red Schoendienst
46. Tom Seaver
47. Duke Snider
48. Joe Torre
49. Bill Veeck
50. Carl Yastrzemski

INTRODUCTION

George Vass

As a youngster growing up in Springfield, Illinois, in the early 1940s, I had the pleasure of being able to read regularly the famous Blue Streak Edition of the now defunct *Chicago Daily News* (believe it or not, in those days the Daily News was delivered to your door in Springfield, which is about 200 miles southwest of Chicago, excepting Sundays when—another believe it or not—the paper wasn't published).

While even at a tender age I appreciated being able to follow the events of World War II as reported by the newspaper's wide-flung Foreign News Service, I was even more intrigued by the sports pages, which featured such writing luminaries as columnist John P. Carmichael and sports editor Lloyd Lewis, the latter of whom also was a noted Civil War historian.

One of the most memorable features of the sports section was an extended series of first-person, as-told-to stories called *"My Greatest Day in Baseball."* The vast majority of them were written by Carmichael, who had an exceptional talent for relating anecdotes, as well as enabling the subjects of his interviews to tell their stories in their own way, in their individual accents, so to speak.

In that wonderful series, he and several other contributors, including Lewis, served as "conduits" to enable such great old-time players as Ty Cobb, Honus Wagner, Clark Griffith, Tris Speaker and dozens of others to relate in their own words their most memorable games and on-the-field experiences. Eventually, these stories were published in book form in a collection that has been reprinted several times.

The series *"My Greatest Day in Baseball"* was a thrilling education in the game's history from the turn of the century into the early 1940s. It was a virtual seminar, a series of stimulating lectures in newsprint as delivered by those who played major roles in some of the game's most dramatic moments. Their highly personal accounts—which happily often included emotional reactions—of some of baseball's most notable incidents made fascinating reading, often far surpassing in vivid style and detail the objective and relatively dry accounts of the sportswriters who perforce had to look on as outsiders at the events unfolding before them.

No one knows the game, and its ins-and-outs, more intimately than those who participate, and that was readily apparent in this series with all its colorful and revealing anecdotal material as related by the individuals directly involved. It was a revelation, and nurtured a revolution in sports writing, eventually leading to many fine books based on similar oral histories.

In the late 1950s, I became a colleague of Carmichael as a member of the sports staff of *The Chicago Daily News*, and found him as amiable and helpful as his writing philosophy and approach suggested. He might well have taken as a motto a portion of Lincoln's second inaugural address because he wrote his daily column, *The Barber Shop*, with "malice towards none," steadfastly eschewing controversy and negativism. Since he was probably the finest sports columnist in Chicago's long journalistic history, the method may have much to recommend it even in this more antagonistic age.

Another of my colleagues at the *Daily News* was John Kuenster, who already was an outstanding baseball beat writer when I arrived at the paper. Kuenster eventually moved on to other fields of endeavor, and to my surprise I was entrusted with one of the then much-coveted baseball beats in 1965, and hung on to the job until the sad demise of the *Daily News* in 1978.

I began contributing stories to *Baseball Digest* magazine, the oldest surviving monthly publication devoted to baseball, in 1965, almost simultaneously with being assigned the baseball beat on the *Daily News*. Two years later, Kuenster became editor of the magazine, and eventually conceived the notion of a series similar to the onetime *Daily News* feature, this time called *"The Game I'll Never Forget,"* which made its first appearance in the June 1969 issue. Kuenster's inspiration proved fortunate because the new series quickly became one of the most popular features of *Baseball Digest*.

Somehow, though a handful of the articles were written by others, I quickly stumbled into a virtual monopoly of doing them during the 26 years (1969–95) the series ran in the magazine. In preparing this collection of 50 first-hand accounts being offered in this book I was stunned to discover that over a quarter of a century I had conducted 279 interviews to write 279 as told-to stories in the series. (And there are several dozen more I contributed to *Hockey Digest*, a sister magazine).

It was a wonderful experience to uncover what so many of the players of the last 30 years—and sometimes earlier—considered their most memorable games, sometimes diverging sharply from the ones you would expect them to choose. It was an education in baseball as well as in its history to hear Mickey Mantle, Carl Yastrzemski, Willie Mays, Tony Conigliaro, Bill Veeck, Frank Lane and hundreds of other famous and not-so-famous players tell their stories, and explain why a certain game so vividly and indelibly impressed itself in their memories.

That makes it all the more of a privilege and a joy to be able to pass on their stories in a more permanent form just as Carmichael and his colleagues of half a century ago preserved the recollections of an earlier generation of great players.

November 10, 1998

WALTER ALSTON

Despite the briefest of major league careers as a player, striking out in his only at-bat, the unflappable and almost colorless Walter Alston ranks among the greatest and most durable of managers. He led the Brooklyn-Los Angeles Dodgers in a quiet but authoritative style for 23 seasons (1954–76), his teams winning seven National League pennants and four World Series.

Maybe it's the way I look at a game that makes it difficult for me to pick out one and say, "That's the one I'll never forget."

The games that satisfy me the most are the ones I've made the right moves in as a manager, the ones that I can be sure I did everything I could to win even if we lost. Every move a manager makes doesn't work out, but the important thing is that you made the right ones.

Managing a big league ball club calls for a lot of decisions. You are going to make some wrong ones. The important thing is you make more that work for you than against you.

It's the problem-solving that gives me satisfaction. The right answer isn't always the obvious one. You've got to take a lot of things into account in every close game, including the personalities of the players, their strengths, their weaknesses, as well as those of the men on the other team.

Fear of being second-guessed has never bothered me. I've always tried to arrive at a decision on a logical basis and then stick with it. The next day I might analyze what happened, how it worked out, but only in order to use the information some other time, to learn.

When you ask me which game pleased me most it might well be the one we played yesterday because we did everything right. I made a pitching change that got us out of a jam, I got a little lucky. I could be satisfied with my managing.

There are many games I remember in some detail, games from which I've learned something. One of the most difficult decisions I ever had to make was whether to pitch Sandy Koufax or Don Drysdale in the seventh game of the 1965 World Series against the Minnesota Twins.

Everything hung on that game with the Series tied 3–3, and I had to choose whether to send Koufax, a left-hander, or Drysdale, a right-hander, against the Twins. Drysdale had three days of rest, Koufax had only two and had had an arthritic elbow all season.

I knew Koufax could pitch with only two days of rest despite his elbow problem. And the Twins were more vulnerable to left-handed pitching. I started Koufax and he won 2–0. It was a decision I had no reason to regret, but even if we had lost it it would have been the right one.

Take the seventh game of the 1955 World Series against the New York Yankees, the first one the Brooklyn Dodgers ever won. That's one to remember, the one in which Johnny Podres pitched a 2–0 shutout.

Podres pitched great ball, but it wasn't an easy game. It never is with just two runs and the Yankees got their share of hits (eight, including two doubles, on October 4, 1955, at Yankee Stadium).

It was a game in which I had a lot of decisions to make, though I suppose that's true of most. This time they all worked with some luck to help out.

We scored our second run in the sixth inning, and I tried for more by sending up George Shuba, a left-handed hitter, to bat for Don Zimmer, against Bob Grim a right-handed pitcher. Shuba made the third out, and I had to make some defensive changes for the Yankee half of the sixth.

I moved Junior Gilliam from left field to second base in place of Zimmer, and sent Sandy Amoros to left because he was a better defensive outfielder than Shuba.

The Yankees got the first two men on base, and that brought up Yogi Berra in a situation in which a hit could put them back into the game.

Berra hit a high fly ball toward the left field corner. Amoros was playing him shaded to center, and the ball looked as if it might drop in for a double to tie the game.

Amoros had to make a long run to even get near the ball and the Yankees thought it couldn't possibly be caught. Billy Martin took off from second and Gil McDougald from first.

Somehow, Amoros got to the ball, reaching for it with a last-second lunge and catching it just a few inches off the ground as it was about to hit in fair territory.

For a split-second it looked like we might get a triple play. Martin, though, managed to get back to second in time. But Amoros' throw to shortstop Pee Wee Reese was relayed in time to Gil Hodges at first to double up McDougald. The next batter, Hank Bauer, grounded out, and we were out of the inning.

I was conscious I'd made the right move by sending Amoros to left instead of Shuba, but there was also a little luck involved.

If Gilliam had remained in left field it's unlikely he could have made the catch on Berra's ball because he was a right-handed thrower with the glove on his left hand. Amoros was a left-handed thrower with the glove on his right hand, and so could reach for the ball.

Clearly, that was the most important play of the game, and the key one in the Series. If Berra's ball had dropped in for a double both runs would have scored, tying the game 2–2, and who can tell what would have happened.

In that case luck—that of having Amoros in the right place at the right time—had a great deal to do with us winning the game. You can't ever understate the part that luck plays in baseball.

But the decisions a manager makes every inning, every game, have a lot to do with the outcome, too. And through the years, that was the pleasure of managing for me. Each game is memorable in its own way, and most satisfying when you feel you made the greatest percentage of "right" decisions.

Photo by Ron Mrowiec

LUIS APARICIO

A great fielding shortstop from Venezuela, Hall of Famer Luis Aparicio was still playing regularly at the age of 38 in his 17th season as a big leaguer in 1972. The American League Rookie of the Year for 1956 with the Chicago White Sox also was an offensive force, especially on the basepaths. He led the American League in stolen bases nine times.

I've been in the major leagues since 1956 when I came up to the Chicago White Sox and I think I can play two or three more years.

Maybe I can hold onto my job long enough so my son, Luis III, can take my place. He's 15 now and a pretty good shortstop already. It would be really something if that could happen. You know, I took my father's place at shortstop on the Maracaibo (Venezuela) team, November 18, 1954.

In the 18 years since then there have been two games I'll never forget. One was with the Baltimore Orioles in 1966 and I was just out there on the field watching Paul Blair catch the fly, ending the World Series. No one could believe that Baltimore had beaten the Los Angeles Dodgers four games in a row.

The other game was with the Chicago White Sox in 1959, when we won the American League pennant for the first time in 40 years.

Nobody had expected us to win the pennant because we didn't have the power of some other teams, like the New York Yankees and Cleveland Indians. The Yankees, like always, were supposed to have the edge. They had won the pennant four years in a row, and nine of the past 10 seasons.

We didn't have the kind of players the Yankees had—Mickey Mantle, Yogi Berra, Hank Bauer, Elston Howard, guys like that—but we had a good team. We had Nellie Fox at second base, Sherm Lollar catching, Jim Rivera, Jim Landis and Al Smith in the outfield.

We had good speed and some fine pitchers, like Billy Pierce, Dick Donovan, Bob Shaw, Early Wynn, and guys like Gerry Staley and Turk Lown in the bullpen.

We got off to a good start, won our first four games, and surprised everyone by staying in first place almost all the way. We'd steal a game here, squeeze another one out there, and play just good enough to win almost every day.

Maybe it should have been a tip off when we won the opener at Detroit on a home run in the 14th inning by Nellie Fox. Nellie wasn't a player to hit many home runs but he could beat you a lot of other ways, and he earned the Most Valuable Player Award that year.

As I said, we were never hot—winning 10, 12 games in a row, or anything like that. We just kept winning, getting by by a run. Won three games here, lost one, won four more, lost two. Real steady. We won 33 games by the margin of one run.

I think the most important series we won was in late August. We went into Cleveland 1½ games ahead of them with four games to play in the series. We won all four games, and we left Cleveland 5½ games ahead of the Indians, and they were the closest club to us.

After that, we were pretty confident we would win the pennant, but you're never sure of that until it says in the standings that you've done it.

Our chance to clinch the pennant came on Tuesday, September 22, 1959. We played the Indians again in Cleveland. We were 3½ games ahead of them. We had four games left to play and they had five, so they still had a mathematical chance. If we won, it was all over.

Early Wynn started for us and Jim Perry, a rookie that year, for the Indians. The Indians got the first chance to score in the second inning when they got Minnie Minoso to third base and Russ Nixon on first with Rocky Colavito at bat and just one out.

Colavito hit a flyball to left field along the line. Al Smith made the catch at a bad angle but he threw a strike to the plate and Minoso was out trying to score. It might have been a different game if Smitty hadn't made the good throw. But he'd been making it all season.

We got to Perry in the second inning. Bubba Phillips got a single to center and I hit a double off the right field wall to score him. Then Billy Goodman got me across with another double.

The Indians got a run in the fifth inning off Wynn on a walk and singles by Gordie Coleman and Jim Piersall to make it 2–1.

The Indians took out Perry for a pinch hitter in the fifth, so Mudcat Grant started the sixth inning for them. Smitty hit his first pitch over the fence in left. The next batter, Rivera, also hit a homer, and we were ahead 4–1.

Wynn had thrown a lot of pitches by the sixth inning and when the Indians got another run off him, to make it 4–2, Al Lopez [Sox manager] took him out. Bob Shaw got out of trouble that inning, and in the seventh and eighth.

But the Indians kept coming. With one out in the ninth, they loaded the bases on Shaw. The third guy to get on was Piersall, who got a single off Fox's glove. A single would tie the game, and the next batter was Vic Power, a real good hitter.

Lopez brought in Gerry Staley to pitch to Power. Staley had a great sinker, and he was as effective that year as any relief pitcher I've ever seen.

Staley threw just one pitch. It was a sinker, and Power hit it on the ground right to me at shortstop. The ball was hit real hard, and I saw there was plenty of time so I ran over to second, touched the bag, and threw to first to Ted Kluszewski for the doubleplay.

I don't remember exactly what happened after that. Everybody was hollering and slapping each other on the back. We'd won the pennant and were on our way to the World Series.

The trip back to Chicago after the game was one wild party. There was a big mob of fans at Midway Airport to welcome us, and it's a good thing we didn't have a game the next day.

Everybody wasn't happy. A lot of people were mad that somebody had ordered the air raid sirens in Chicago set off a few minutes after we'd won the pennant. I guess a lot of people thought there really was an air raid.

But I didn't learn about that 'til later. All I know is that when I stepped on second base and threw to first we won the pennant.

Photo by Ron Mrowiec

ERNIE BANKS

The most popular of all Chicago Cubs, Ernie Banks was a standout both as a shortstop and then as a first baseman. He ranks among the top home run hitters of all time with 512 during his 19–season career (1953–71), all spent with the Cubs. Known as Mr. Cub, he hit a career-high of 47 home runs in 1958, and was twice chosen as the National League's Most Valuable Player.

I don't have any trouble picking out the game I'll never forget even though I've seen a lot of ball games since and had quite a few thrills. But this was such an unusual game that anybody who was there would have to remember quite a bit about it.

It was the game in which Sam Jones pitched what I call an unusual-type no-hitter against the Pittsburgh Pirates for the Cubs at Wrigley Field. I know you'd call any no-hitter unusual, but this was more so than any I've seen and I have seen a few.

The reason I say that is because Jones was extremely wild during the game, and he did not have what you would call a good fielding team behind him. But every pitch it seemed like you would have to make a good play to save the no-hitter.

I was playing shortstop at the time, which was on May 12, 1955, and the Pirates had a good hitting team with Nelson King pitching for them against us. Sam Jones had been with Cleveland before he came to the Cubs. He was called Toothpick Sam because he always had a toothpick in his mouth while he was pitching.

He was known at the time he joined the Cubs as a wild pitcher. His control was a big problem but he had a good arm and a great curve ball. He was always a pitcher that you figured if he had fairly good control he would win—but on that day he had real bad control yet pitched a no-hitter.

It was a sunny, warm day, and yet there wasn't much of a crowd when the game started. And as it went on they really didn't get very excited because nobody really thought Toothpick Sam would finish. Everybody figured he would be taken out anytime.

I guess he ran the count to 3–2 on about nine batters, and he did walk seven when it was all over. It seemed like he was always in trouble on every pitch, but just when you thought he was gone he'd strike out a man— wait 'til I tell you about the ninth inning.

The Pirates started King, and we got a run off him in the first inning and then again in the second. I remember getting a triple off Vern Law in the fifth inning to score our third run, and we scored another run later in the game on a home run.

While we were doing a lot of hitting, Toothpick Sam was struggling along. The Pirates were a good-hitting team with Dick Groat, Roberto Clemente, Frank Thomas, Dale Long and George Freese in the lineup, so it was no easy job for Toothpick Sam to get them out.

But he kept doing it. I remember Long walked in the second inning, but our catcher, Clyde McCullough, threw him out trying to steal second base. Gene Baker was playing second for us, and he and I made a couple of doubleplays to get out of jams.

Those two double plays were the main plays that created excitement because Sam needed them to get out of a couple of innings. One ball was hit near the second base bag, and I was able to get over to it and feed it to Baker for the doubleplay. And Baker started another one.

There was maybe one great play in the field—or at least it was a good play. That was when Freese hit the ball deep to center field and Eddie Miksis, who was playing out there for us, made a leaping, one-handed catch of the ball.

It was that sort of thing that made it so unusual a game for me. We had a fairly slow team, and our outfield wasn't exactly what you'd call fast or strong defensively.

Miksis, who had been an infielder, was playing center field. Bob Speake was in left, and Ted Tappe in right field. I guess Tappe hit the homer. But it wasn't what you'd think of as a defensive outfield, and yet here was Toothpick Sam getting a no-hitter when you would think he'd need great speed and a lot of good plays behind him to do it.

But he kept walking men and striking them out, and before we knew it he was in the ninth inning with the no-hitter going although nobody expected him to last that long. All he had to do was get out the heart of the batting order with the bases loaded because he started out by walking the first three Pirates in the inning.

So here were Groat, Clemente and Thomas coming up with three men on. Our manager, Stan Hack, went out to talk to Sam, and told him to get the ball over. Later, Hack said he was going to take him out if he walked another man

But Toothpick Sam just threw as hard as he could and struck out Groat, Clemente, and Thomas in order, and that was the no-hitter. When we went up to congratulate him, he said he hadn't even realized he had one until we started slapping him on the back and yelling about it.

It was so unusual that you couldn't believe he had pitched a no-hitter, but he had, and the television station, WGN-TV, presented him later with a gold toothpick to commemorate the game.

There were some other things that made it unusual. It was the first no-hitter ever pitched by a black man in the major leagues. And it was the first no-hitter pitched in Wrigley Field in almost 40 years. The last one before that had been in 1917 when Jim Vaughn and Fred Toney had pitched a double no-hitter.

It was just so unusual all the way around. Wrigley Field is the last place you would expect a no-hitter—although there've been some since—especially for a pitcher who was wild, and with a slow team behind him.

But that's a game I'll never forget. It was just so unexpected.

Photo courtesy of Oakland A's

VIDA BLUE

Few pitchers have gotten off to such sensational starts as left-hander Vida Blue, who helped the Oakland A's to three consecutive (1972–74) World Series titles. In his first full major league season of 1971 Blue's record was 24–8, and he won the Cy Young Award as well as led the American League with an earned run average of 1.82. He was a 20–game winner three times in a career that extended from 1969 to 1986.

The most memorable game in my career is the no-hitter I pitched as a rookie just after being called up by the Oakland A's in 1970 because I think it's something every pitcher dreams of from a personal standpoint.

For most pitchers, I'm sure that the most memorable game would be one they won in a playoff, one in which their team clinched the pennant, or one they won in a World Series. I can appreciate that because I've been fortunate enough to pitch in the playoffs and in the World Series several times. But for me, personally, the game I'll never forget is that no-hitter because of the circumstances, and because it happened at the outset of my career.

It was late in the 1970 season that I was called up by the A's, and I got a start Labor Day against the White Sox in Chicago. I didn't pitch well and, though we won the game, I wasn't the winning pitcher. But I did hit a home run with two men on before I was knocked out in the fifth inning. I was trying too hard, and I kept telling myself next time I had to just be myself, pitch my own game.

The next start came four days later against the Royals at Kansas City and this time I had nothing to blame myself for. I did pitch my own game, and it foreshadowed what was to come. I decided to pitch the way I'd pitched in the minors on the way up, to show 'em my curve ball just enough to make the batters careful, and then to try and blow the ball past them.

It worked for me, even better than I could have expected. In the fifth inning I realized I had a no-hitter going, and it made me nervous. I got wild. I was telling myself to just pitch, just throw the ball. It got better when we scored a run, and I thought I might just pitch a no-hitter that game.

Well, it wasn't to be that night. It went into the eighth inning with two outs, then Pat Kelly lined a single. I was disappointed. But I just told myself, "It's gone. Nothing I could do about it. Get back to work." And I did. Kelly's hit was the only one, and we won the game 3–0.

I didn't feel too bad after the game, losing the no-hitter. I felt I'd accomplished something, proved something, and that I'd have to and would do it again. There'd be other chances for no-hitters.

What I didn't dream was how soon that would come, just two starts later, in Oakland against the Minnesota Twins (September 21, 1970).

The Twins were trying to clinch the American League West Division title that night—as they did later—and Jim Perry was pitching for them. They had a good lineup, good hitters, Harmon Killebrew, Tony Oliva, Cesar Tovar.

I felt particularly good that day, particularly strong. I planned to pitch to the Twins just as I'd done to the Royals in the one-hitter, strength against strength, mostly fast balls, just showing the curve.

That day I had exceptionally good stuff, exceptionally good control, all pitches were just very accurate, and I pinpointed the ball. I went one batter from having a perfect game.

We scored a run in the first inning, and that's the way it stayed until the eighth, which might have helped me. I knew I couldn't afford to get careless with a one-run lead. I retired the first 11 batters, but I was too careful with Killebrew in the fourth and walked him. He was the one man I was afraid of. He hit the ball a long way. I didn't want him to tie the game with one swing.

In the sixth, George Mitterwald ripped a liner toward left, but Campy Campaneris (shortstop) leaped and backhanded it. That was one of the two balls hit hard by the 28 batters I faced in that game.

Believe it or not, in such a game where a pitcher dominates throughout there still has to be a lot of luck in the positioning of the defense. But I made a lot of good pitches inside and outside. I had the hitters off balance, and that's what pitching is all about. I had very good control and good velocity both at the same time. And I was in rhythm.

Most pitchers, when they're pitching well, whether they pitch a no-hitter or just win the game, get into a rhythm where you just get the ball from the catcher and throw it back. You have a feeling for the pitches.

Most of the time I like to have the catcher call 35 to 40 percent of the pitches, which is what Gene Tenace did that day. A lot of times you see a pitcher shake the catcher off, but I would say a good 25 percent of the time that's just a decoy to make the batter think about another pitch. It might make the difference of a guy hitting the ball to the warning track as compared to hitting it over the fence. In this game, I just had the feel for the pitches, and everything the catcher called I threw. It's amazing how sometimes it works like that.

By the fifth inning I was thinking about the no-hitter. How could I help it? I thought about the one I'd lost. It was early, but I didn't want to do that again. Still, I didn't want to get nervous. I didn't even think about the superstition of not having anyone mention it. It was early in my career and I wasn't even aware of it. Now I know if I ever get close to a no-hitter again I'm going to be aware. But I don't think it'll be up to me to say, "Sh--, don't say anything—I have a no-hitter."

I know the announcers are more superstitious than anyone else. I've seen them on television referring to a pitcher who has retired 15 batters in a row in five innings, and they'll say, "You know what that means . . . you see the 'graphics' right there. We'll be right back after this message."

No one mentioned it to me that day, and luckily it did turn out right for me. We got five runs in the eighth, and went into the ninth leading 6–0. I'd retired 13 batters in a row and had only three to go for the no-hitter. I was very nervous, and I had made up my mind just to throw hard. I struck out Danny Thompson, then Bob Allison. The next batter was Tovar, who could handle the bat. I was so nervous I could hardly throw the ball.

I got two strikes on him, then threw a fast ball up and away. He popped it foul, and Don Mincher (first baseman) got under it and put it away. I had my no-hitter. This time it didn't get away.

That was my most memorable game, though I was involved in another no-hitter five years later. That was the combination no-hitter in which I pitched the first five innings against the California Angels (September 28, 1975) and three other pitchers—Glenn Abbott, Paul Lindblad, and Rollie Fingers—pitched the rest.

We were getting ready for the championship playoffs, we had clinched the division, so I did not at all mind leaving the game after having pitched the allotted number of innings to qualify for the victory. Besides, it was late in September, and the football season had started. It was a Sunday afternoon and, being a very avid football fan, I wanted to go home and watch a game on TV.

In fact, I didn't even think about a no-hitter until I got home and while watching the football game somebody told me I'd been involved in a combination no-hit game.

But that was nothing like the no-hitter I pitched by myself.

Photo courtesy of San Francisco Giants

BOBBY BONDS

An unusual blend of great speed and exceptional power, as well as a strong throwing arm, made Bobby Bonds one of the finest lead-off men and outfielders during his career (1968–81), much of it flanking Willie Mays for the San Francisco Giants. Bonds five times topped 30 home runs and 30 stolen bases in one season. His peak output was in 1973 when he batted .283 with 39 home runs, 131 runs scored, 96 runs batted in, and 43 stolen bases.

I have so many, and I mean so many, memories of the game that it's difficult to pick and choose about which has been my biggest thrill.

Right from the start, the very day I broke into the big leagues with the San Francisco Giants, I had something to remember. I was called up from Phoenix, where I'd been having a real good year (.367) in mid-season 1968, and the Giants put me into the lineup right away, in right field.

You can imagine the feeling that was for a kid, to be playing next to Willie Mays, who was in center field, and on a club that had Willie McCovey at first base, Juan Marichal on the pitching staff, as well as some other outstanding players.

We were playing the Los Angeles Dodgers at Candlestick Park (June 25, 1968). I remember Claude Osteen was pitching for the Dodgers, and that I grounded out in my first at-bat. The second time up I got hit by a pitch. But it's the third big league at-bat that I remember.

The bases were loaded, and the Dodgers had a relief pitcher, John Purdin, in the game. It's been a long time, so I don't remember the exact pitch, but I hit it good. A grand slam in my first major league game! It's a memory to treasure because no other big leaguer in modern major league history has ever hit a grand slam in his first game, though I believe one player did it in the 1890s.

So there's one big memory. Another comes from an All-Star game. That's the one in 1973 at Kansas City. I got into that game in the fourth inning, and in the fifth, my first time at bat, I hit a home run for the National League off Bill Singer. A couple of innings later, I got a double, so I was 2–for–3 in that game in which we beat the American League, 7–1.

But I guess the biggest one that sticks out, strangely enough, is a game I didn't play in because I was injured. That game stands out because it's the one in which we clinched the National League West Division championship in San Francisco. Not was it the only championship I've ever been involved in in the big leagues, but it's the closest I've ever gotten to a World Series. So that always will be a memento to me.

In some ways, 1971 may have been my best year, and it certainly was the best for the Giants in the seven years I was with them. I hit .288 that year, drove in more than a 100 runs, and hit over 30 homers. And the club got off to a real good start, winning something like 35 of their first 50 games.

All the same, injuries started catching up with us late in the season and the Dodgers were right on our heels going into the final days. We were just a game ahead of them going into the last series of the year. We played the Padres at San Diego while the Dodgers played Houston at Los Angeles.

Believe it or not, we had a lot of trouble with San Diego that year. We could not beat San Diego and we could not beat Montreal, two recent expansion teams. We handled the veteran clubs much easier for some reason. We could beat the Dodgers and we could beat the Cincinnati Reds, but we had trouble with the clubs at the bottom. We would have preferred to play a tougher ball club in a series on which the divisional title depended.

Both the Dodgers and we won the first games so were still a game ahead with now just two left to play. The next to the last game I was really hurting. I'd had a rib cage injury, and on a play sliding into second I couldn't breathe. But Charlie Fox, our manager, said, "We need you. You've got to play. Play as long as you can."

I was in there about five innings. But I could hardly swing the bat or run so I had to leave the game. And what a game it was! It went 10 innings, and the Padres beat us 4–1. Luckily, the Astros also beat the Dodgers that night so we still had a one game lead with one game to go.

We'd clinched at least a tie for the division title, but we didn't want to share it, to have an extra playoff. We wanted to make sure by winning outright. Besides, some people had been saying all year we were going to blow it. They were maybe thinking about all those second place finishes, five in a row, the Giants had had in recent years.

The situation being what it was, we felt we had to win that game from San Diego, and not to take any chances, Juan Marichal, our best pitcher, had to start. We couldn't go with our second best or third best pitcher, though we would have preferred to save Marichal so he could start twice in the (league) championship series.

So Marichal started. But I wasn't in the lineup. I wanted to be in the game. I tested myself, but my rib cage was so sore. I had such a hard time even breathing that I would have hurt the club more by playing than by staying on the bench. It killed me, but I sat the game out.

The way things happened, the guy who replaced me had a tremendous game, so I had no regrets. Manager Fox put Dave Kingman, a rookie who had been with the club only two months, into right field (September 30, 1971). All he did was hit a two-run homer in the fourth off Dave Roberts, the Padres pitcher. That came after Mays had driven in the first run with a double.

Marichal pitched just a tremendous game, a five-hitter, and we won 5–1, and clinched the division title on the last day of the season.

I've never been in a celebration like that one. It was the greatest thrill of my life, after all we'd gone through, after the way we'd hung in there despite the injuries, despite the problems. And the enthusiasm of the players. Mays, McCovey, and the great game Marichal pitched, was a tremendous experience. To be associated with such great players, well, that's something to remember all your life in itself.

So that's the game I'll never forget, and it's bound to be the one unless I happen to be lucky enough to get into a World Series.

LOU BOUDREAU

It's impossible to conceive that any player, especially a player-manager, ever met the challenge of rising to the occasion so spectacularly as did Hall of Fame shortstop Lou Boudreau in a pivotal game. Called the "Boy Manager" when he was appointed by the Cleveland Indians at the age of 24 in 1942, Boudreau led his team to a pennant in 1948 with his play as much as his strategy. He managed several other teams before becoming a radio commentator on the game.

Oh yes, I really hate to talk about that game. You have to twist my arm to get me to tell you about it. I don't know what it is, but people have been asking about the 1948 American League playoff game for more than 30 years now, and somehow I've forced myself to tell the story over and over again.

When you've been in baseball as long as I have you tend to forget that a lot of fans have come along who are too young to remember the 1948 season, or weren't even born at the time. That's the great thing about baseball, its continuing appeal. New fans, new memories.

I've got a lot of great memories, but 1948 was something special. That year we set an attendance record in Cleveland with more than 2,600,000 fans turning out to watch the Indians. Bill Veeck, who ran the club, was a wonder at getting people to come out to the ballpark and have fun, and they did.

We had a great season on the field as well as at the gate, though the one usually goes with the other. We were in a three-way pennant fight with the New York Yankees and the Boston Red Sox right to the end. We could have clinched the pennant by winning our last game, but we lost as the Red Sox beat the Yankees to earn a tie.

That set up the first championship playoff in the history of the American League. It was just one game, at Boston on October 4, 1948. That's easily the most important game of my career, both as a player and as manager. In fact, nobody knew better than I did that my job as manager of the Indians hung on the outcome of that game. I was convinced Veeck was ready to trade me or buy up my contract as manager if we didn't win the pennant.

Not too many people thought we'd beat the Red Sox in that playoff game. We had to handcuff such hitters as Ted Williams, Junior Stephens, Bobby Doerr, Stan

Spence and Johnny Pesky. A tough assignment for any pitcher.

The day before the game, I held a club meeting to outline my pitching plans, which I figured might surprise some people. I explained that at the moment Gene Bearden was my best pitcher, better than Bob Feller, better than Bob Lemon, better than Steve Gromek. I was starting Bearden, and if anybody had any objections or suggestions I wanted to hear them.

The players backed me up completely. They realized, as I did, that Bearden had a good knuckleball. If he could control it, it would be hard for the Red Sox sluggers to pull into the left field screen or over the short left field wall at Fenway Park.

I asked the players to keep the decision to start Bearden a secret. The Red Sox were starting Denny Galehouse, and let everybody know about it, but I kept the suspense up to the last moment. I warmed up Bearden, Feller and Lemon right before the game. In any case, I wanted Feller and Lemon ready if Bearden ran into trouble.

Even now, it's hard to believe what happened that day. Because of the importance of the game, what it meant to so many people, and its impact on my entire career, that game has to rank at the top of my long list of thrills. It was a game in which I could do nothing wrong.

The first inning should have been an indication of the way things were going. Galehouse got the first two batters out and I was up. I let two bad balls go by, fouled off the third, then hit a long fly ball that hit the screen over the left field wall, good for a home run to put us ahead 1–0.

The Red Sox got that run back quickly. They scored on a double by Pesky and a single by Stephens, and we went into the fourth inning tied 1–1.

I led off the fourth inning with a single, and Joe Gordon moved me to second with another single. Ken Keltner was at bat and I could have played it safe by ordering a sacrifice bunt, the orthodox thing to do. But it was early in the game, and I decided to go for the big inning and let Keltner "hit away."

I was a "genius" that day. Keltner hit the ball as far as he could, over the left field wall for his 31st home run of the season, with two men on, to give us a 4–1 lead.

When I stepped on home plate and waited to shake Keltner's hand I felt like turning somersaults. We were three runs ahead and Bearden was pitching like a poised veteran. The pressure now was all on the Red Sox, with a pennant at stake.

We got another run that inning, then I hit my second home run of the game in the fifth to put us ahead 6–1.

The Red Sox gave it all they had. They scored two runs in the sixth when Williams hit a home run with a man on. But I stayed with Bearden. He still had a three-run lead, and I felt confident he could hold Boston the rest of the way.

We added to our lead with single runs in the eighth and ninth. I managed a single in my last turn at bat. That gave me a perfect day, two home runs, two singles and an intentional walk.

We carried an 8–3 lead into the Boston half of the ninth. It was an easy inning as Bearden, stronger at the finish than at the start, retired the last three batters without trouble.

When third baseman Keltner fielded Birdie Tebbetts' grounder and threw to Eddie Robinson at first for the final out, I rushed to the box where my wife, Della, was sitting. I hardly knew what to say to her, so I grabbed her, kissed her as hard as I could.

We'd won the pennant. Veeck, ignoring his artificial leg, jumped over the railing of his box, ran across the field, and caught up with us players as we streamed into the locker room. He didn't say much, but the way he gripped my hand told me how he felt.

No, don't ask me about that game. I hate to talk about it. Even now, after more than 30 years, it's hard to believe what happened, and the way it happened.

There's no way I can ever forget a detail of that game.

Photo courtesy of Atlanta Braves

ORLANDO CEPEDA

The "Baby Bull" or "Cha-Cha" as he was alternately nick-named, was a formidable slugger who played vital roles on pennant-winning teams at San Francisco and St. Louis during a career that extended from 1958 to 1974. In 1961 he batted .311 with 46 home runs and 142 runs batted in. Most of his 379 career home runs came as a first baseman.

I've been lucky enough to play in three World Series, once with the San Francisco Giants in 1962, and twice with the St. Louis Cardinals, in 1967 and 1968. That gives me a few games from which to pick the World Series Game I'll Never Forget.

It is not difficult for me to forget most of the games of the 1962 Series between the Giants and the New York Yankees because I got a hit in only one of the five in which I played. That was the sixth game, which the Giants won, before losing the seventh game and the championship to the Yankees.

The sixth game was a good one for me and the Giants. Billy Pierce pitched for us and Whitey Ford for the Yankees. I got lucky and had a good day. I got a double and drove in a run, and also scored when we got three runs off Ford in the fourth inning. I also drove in a run with a single later in the game, which we won 5–2.

I got three hits in that game so maybe I should think of it as the Series game most important to me, but I don't.

I even remember that when I was at bat in the fourth inning, Felipe Alou was on second base and Willie Mays on first, and Ford tried to pick Alou off the bag. But he threw the ball into center field and Alou scored, and Mays went to third. That's when I got the double which I think was my first hit in the Series after going out 13 times.

It was a good game for me, but then we lost the Series the next day—you remember the tremendous line drive Willie McCovey hit to Bobby Richardson for the last out—so it did not mean anything so big. When you lose it does not make you too happy.

When I think about it, the Series game I'll never forget would have to be the seventh game of the 1967 World Series. You might look at the box score and wonder why I pick that one. It shows I got no hits and I was at bat five times.

I'll tell you why that seventh game is the one I'll never forget. It is because we won it, we beat the Boston Red Sox to bring the championship to St. Louis. It was more important to me than anything because it made complete for me the whole year, the good year, the best I could have.

It was very important for me because the Giants traded me the year before—they did not want me, and now I helped St. Louis win the championship.

The Giants traded me to St. Louis early in the 1966 season. I was very shocked. I had been there with them for many years and then I hurt my knee. I was operated on in December 1964, and it took a long time to heal. I could not play very much in 1965, and then when 1966 started the Giants could not use me. I wanted to be traded. I asked them to do so. But I felt hurt when they did.

They didn't want me, they didn't need me, they could not use me, so I forgot about them. I turned my back on them and I became a Cardinal. I knew I could help them. I think I did the first year, 1966, when I was with them (Cepeda batted .301, and was voted Comeback of the Year).

The next year is the one I'll never forget. For myself, it was a very good year, but more important it was so for the Cardinals. We won the pennant in 1967, and it was because we were a very good team at every position, and there was great harmony. There was no jealousy on the team. We all worked together.

I feel real proud about that year. It is not only because I won the Most Valuable Player Award—and got all the votes—but because it was a year in which the team won the championship. (Cepeda was chosen MVP unanimously after batting .325 with 25 home runs and 111 runs batted in.)

It also made me feel good because I had been traded and the Giants could no longer use me yet I had helped the Cardinals. They had been able to use me, they wanted me, and they needed me.

I did not get many hits in that World Series against the Boston Red Sox. I did not get any in the first two games. And I wanted to get some when the Series went to a seventh game, which was in Boston. I tried as hard as I could, but I did not.

Yet we knew we would win the seventh game. We had the better team. Bob Gibson started, and he was the best pitcher in baseball. Jim Lonborg pitched for the Red Sox.

We got two runs in the second inning. Dal Maxvill hit a triple. I remember that. And I know later Gibson himself hit a home run. He is a good hitter. But we won the game easily (7–3), and what I remember most is how happy we were afterwards.

We climbed on a table and started doing the singing and the Cha-Cha in the locker room, and the TV and newspaper people came in, and it was very crowded and hot.

I've had better games—I mean I have had hits, home runs and that kind of thing. But that doesn't matter. What meant more was this, that this was the seventh game of a World Series and we had won it.

You never forget that kind of a game. There is nothing like it. I know that is the game I'll never forget. It is different when you win the World Series. It is not like any other game.

Photo courtesy of Los Angeles Dodgers

RON CEY

Nicknamed "Penguin," Ron Cey was more of a bulldog as a power-hitting third baseman. He was part of the longest-lasting infield quartet (with first baseman Steve Garvey, second baseman Davey Lopes, and shortstop Bill Russell) in the game's annals for the Los Angeles Dodgers from 1973 to 1980. Cey hit 316 home runs in 17 seasons (1971–87).

I've been playing a long time, and maybe there's not one game that sticks out. Well, maybe one. But I've got a lot of memories because I played on some good Dodger teams at Los Angeles, and more often than not we were winners, or in the running.

Here are a few games that stand out in my memory:

There was the National League championship playoff game against the Phillies in 1977, the first game (October 4, 1977). We were losing 5–1 in the seventh inning, and Steve Carlton was pitching for the Phillies.

We got the bases loaded in the seventh on a couple of walks and a single by Davey Lopes. I came to bat just looking to keep the rally going, to hit the ball anywhere. The count got up to 3–2 and I knew Carlton wasn't going to give in, that I had to protect the plate. I fouled off one pitch, then another. Then another. The next pitch was up a little, and I got all of it, a grand slam to tie the game.

We didn't win the game—the Phillies got a couple of runs in the ninth, and beat us 7–5—but you never forget coming through in a situation like that. And we did win the playoffs.

Another game was in the 1978 World Series against the New York Yankees, the second game (October 12, 1978, at Yankee Stadium). The year before, in the '77 Series, I'd hit a home run off Catfish Hunter, and he was pitching again.

The Yankees scored a couple of runs in the third inning off Burt Hooton, our starting pitcher. Reggie Jackson drove them in with a double. We got one of those runs back in the fourth when I singled to center field with two men on.

It was still 2–1 in favor of New York in our half of the sixth, and Hunter was still pitching. We had a couple of men on—Lopes and Reggie Smith had singled—when I came to bat.

I don't remember the exact sequence of pitches, but Hunter threw me a slider I know he must have meant to keep away from my power. But it was right over the plate, about belt high, and I hit it over the left-center field wall for a three-run homer.

We went on to win that game 4–3, and I drove in all four runs for us. The odd thing about it was that Jackson drove in all three Yankee runs. A lot of people remember that game because with two out in the ninth and two on Bob Welch had to pitch to Reggie. The count got up to 3–2 and then Welch struck Jackson out to end the game.

That Series was just proof that you never have a lock on anything. We won the first two games—both in New York—but the Yankees won the next four and the Series.

Those are some of the games I remember, and there are many others, big games we won, and even some we lost.

Maybe, though, what I remember most is not just one game, but an entire series, maybe the most important one I ever played in during a regular season. There are a lot of games that are important, but when a pennant hinges on a game or series that has to take precedence over the other ones.

The series I'm talking about is the one at the end of the 1980 season against the Houston Astros. We were three games down with three games to go against the Astros at Los Angeles. We had to win all three games to force a one-game playoff with the Astros for the National League West title.

We hadn't been playing well going into that series. I think we'd lost eight of our last 13 games, but at least we were still alive though we were faced with having to win four straight from the Astros—the three games in the final series, and the one-game playoff.

Every one of those three game to end the season was a struggle. But they were all three great games, and you couldn't ask for a more exciting finish to a division title race.

The series opened Friday night (October 3, 1980) with Ken Forsch pitching for Houston and Don Sutton for us. You couldn't have asked for a tighter game. Each club scored a run in the early innings and it went into the eighth tied 1–1 when Alan Ashby drove in a run for Houston with a sacrifice fly.

The Astros were still leading 2–1 in the bottom of the ninth. We had two men on, two out, and I had two strikes on me. I wasn't swinging well because I'd pulled a hamstring about a week earlier and had even missed the final game of the previous series. But I managed to make contact on Forsch's third pitch and hit a bouncer up the middle that just got through the infield, and it scored Rudy Law with the tying run.

We went on to win that game in extra innings on a homer by Joe Ferguson to stay alive. That was the great thing about that series—you had to win the first game or the rest didn't matter, the same for the second game. There was just no letup.

The second game I went hitless, but we beat the Astros 2–1, Jerry Reuss pitching a great game and Steve Garvey hitting a two-run homer off Nolan Ryan.

That brought it down to the final game of the season, with us one game out. The Astros scored early and it looked pretty dim when they took a 3–0 lead. But we kept pecking away, scoring a run in the third to make it 3–2 going into the bottom of the eighth.

We got a break when Enos Cabell, the Houston third baseman, booted a grounder by Garvey to lead off the inning. I went up to sacrifice, to move Garvey to second, but I fouled off a couple of pitches. The count went to 3–2, and I fouled off another pitch, this time off the top of my foot.

The next pitch by Frank LaCorte was belt high, maybe a little inside, and I hit it into the left-center field pavilion to give us a 4–3 lead. That's the way the game ended. We won it 4–3 to tie for the division title and force the one-game playoff the next day (October 6).

What hurt was that I couldn't play in the playoff against the Astros. When I'd hit that ball off the top of my foot in the at-bat in which I'd hit the home run, I'd caused a blood deposit to form. They'd had to drain it and put an anti-inflammatory drug in it to see if we couldn't get it back in shape as soon as possible because if we won the game against the Astros we'd be going to Philadelphia to play the Phillies in the National League championship series.

But the Astros won the one-game playoff, and it wasn't a close game. They scored early and beat us 7–1.

That's the series I'll never forget. There are other games, many big games I remember. But the ones you remember most are those that mean a great deal, that have magnitude, and that series against Houston fits that description as much as any games I've ever played in.

Photo by Ron Mrowiec

ROBERTO CLEMENTE

The finest right fielder of his era (1955–72), with a rifle throwing arm, and the hitting ability that won four National League batting titles, Roberto Clemente died in an air crash on December 31, 1972, while seeking to help disaster victims in Central America. He finished his career with exactly 3,000 hits, all for the Pittsburgh Pirates. He was elected to the Hall of Fame in 1973.

One game sticks out in my mind, not that there aren't many other big ones to remember. There are a lot of those, but this is the one I'll never forget because I did so good and yet we did not win.

I've said it many times, and I still feel the same way about it. I never go for home runs. I go for hits because I don't believe that you can hit .300 one year and drop to .200 the next. Either you're a good hitter or you are not—unless something is wrong with you physically. Like when I hurt my back in 1957 and hit only .253 after I hit .311 the year before. But if you're a .300 hitter and you're healthy you should hit.

So I don't go for home runs because it is not the way to stay a .300 hitter. But the only thing I think about in hitting is staying strong. If I stay strong I don't have to think about hitting.

When the 1967 season started I felt strong, and I hit more home runs than I usually do. Not because I tried to but because I hit the ball good and it went out of the park.

We were going good after the first month of the 1967 season, and when we went into Cincinnati for a three-game series in mid-May we were right behind the Reds who were in first place. Harry Walker was managing the Pirates and everything was going well, which wasn't the case later in the season.

I was still feeling strong early in the season, and when we went into Cincinnati I think I was hitting .370. At my age—and even then when I was 32—you come to the point where you are tired in the warmer weather. When you are 28 you feel good all the time, but at my age sometimes you feel groggy.

Like I say, this being in May, the weather was still cool, and I know I felt strong in Cincinnati. We had the night game on May 15, and the Reds started Milt Pappas, a good pitcher.

In the first inning, Maury Wills, who was playing shortstop for us, got on base in the first inning, and I came up with a man on. I got around on an outside pitch by Pappas, and I hit it over the right field fence in old Crosley Field for my first home run.

I don't remember what I did my next time at bat—all I know is that I went out. But the third time up, in the fifth inning, Wills was on base again, and this time I hit the ball over the center field fence, which was a long way in the old Cincinnati park. It went right out—it did not hit over the yellow line they had painted out there to show home runs.

So that was two home runs off Pappas, and we were ahead 4–0. It was nothing to excite me—I had hit two home runs in a game before. And nothing I do good ever excites me. The only time I get happy is winning a game. And this game was not yet won.

The Reds scored three runs in the sixth inning so the game was close again. But this was a good day for me and in the seventh inning I came to bat with two men on base and Darrell Osteen now was pitching for the Reds. I hit the ball good again, this time off the fence for a double to drive in two more runs.

Now I had six runs batted in and we were leading 6–3, but the Reds were able to get to our starter, Bob Veale. They knocked him out in the seventh inning when they got two runs, and we ahead just 6–5 going into the ninth inning.

By this time Jerry Arrigo was pitching for the Reds. He got out the first two men to bat for us in the ninth so I came to bat for the fifth time in the game with nobody on base. This time I hit the ball again over the center field fence to give us a 7–5 lead.

I have to admit that this time I felt excited about what I had done. I had never hit three home runs in a game before, and this is something to remember. Three home runs and a double, and I had driven in all seven runs! Yes, this time I was excited about what I had done.

So we had a 7–5 lead when the Reds came to bat in the last of the ninth. But they wouldn't let us win. Tony Perez got a hit, and then Lee May hit a home run to tie the game 7–7 with two outs.

With the score tied and nobody on base the Reds' manager [Dave Bristol] let the pitcher Arrigo bat for himself. He hit the ball good. He hit it hard down the right field line, and it looked for a minute like the ball was going to go over the fence for a home run to win the game.

I got back quickly in right field, all the way to the fence, and I wasn't sure I could reach the ball. But I went up and saved the home run. I did not catch the ball, but I knocked it down with my glove, and it was a double. Luckily, the next guy went out, and we went into extra innings.

So I thought we still had a chance to win, and maybe I could get another chance to bat. But that wasn't to be. In the 10th inning, Tony Perez hit a home run to center field to win the game 8–7, and that robbed me of most of the satisfaction.

This was the biggest day I ever had, and it had to come in a game that we lost. I had three home runs and a double, saved a home run, and drove in all seven of our runs yet we could not win the game.

A couple of years later I again hit three home runs in a game but that does not stick out in my mind like this one we lost to Cincinnati. I think it was my greatest game. Two home runs to center field and one to right field.

I never try for home runs but this time I hit so many and I was really excited. This game has to be the one that sticks out in my mind—doing so well and then losing it. It is strange.

Photo courtesy of Boston Red Sox

TONY CONIGLIARO

Few players have gotten off to more promising starts than outfielder Tony Conigliaro did with the Boston Red Sox. As a rookie, he hit 24 home runs in 1964, and the next year led the American League with 32 at the age of 20. He was apparently headed for greatness until he was struck in the head by a pitched ball in 1967. He was never quite the same player after that. He died at the age of 45 in 1990.

I don't even like to talk about it, the memory is so horrible. I can't stand to think about it, it makes me sick. First there was the blow, the whistling in my ears, the intense, terrible pain.

One moment I was standing at the plate. The next moment I was lying on the ground, and when I came to I wasn't sure what had happened but I couldn't see. My cheekbone was broken. My eye was puffed up.

It was 1967, the year the Boston Red Sox won the pennant. It was a wild race, four teams in it, when we played the California Angels on August 18.

Jack Hamilton, a right-hander, was pitching for the Angels. I got a single off him in the second inning. That raised my average close to .290. I was having a good season, 20 home runs by mid-August, 67 runs batted in. But it all ended in an instant.

When I came to bat again in the fourth inning there were two out, nobody on base. I stepped in there, adjusted my batting helmet, maybe crowding the plate a little as I always did.

Hamilton threw just one pitch. A fast ball? I don't know. I never saw it. They tell me the pitch just got away from him, took off. It must have.

I can't remember the damn thing. Just the terrible ring in my ears, the whistling, the pain. It was intense. I'd never experienced anything like it before. And never since. I want to forget it; try to.

They carried me off the field on a stretcher. I was conscious, and realized what had happened. But it was like a nightmare. I found out later we'd won the game 3–2 but at the time it didn't matter to me. The pain on the left side of my head was terrible.

For the first seven days the eye was closed, and the doctors didn't know what the result would be, how serious the damage was. When the eye opened the doctors discovered that a blister had formed and broken, and it appeared that my vision had been permanently damaged.

Still, there was hope the condition would stabilize. I went to spring training in 1968, but it was clear to me that I couldn't do anything. I couldn't see the ball—I didn't have any depth perception. And when I was examined again, the doctors told me the condition was worsening.

I was shattered when I had to announce in April 1968 that I couldn't play again. I firmly believed it. There was no reason to think I'd ever be able to see well enough to hit. I couldn't talk about baseball. I couldn't even bear to think about it.

I was on the bench (by special permission) for the 1967 World Series with the St. Louis Cardinals. It was rough to sit there and watch without being able to help.

But I still had hope then that by spring I'd be all right. Then when spring training came and I discovered that I still couldn't see well enough to play, that my eye was getting worse, I was shattered.

I went to nightclub singing only to have something to do, something to take my mind off what had happened. Those next few months in 1968 were the worst of my life. I felt as if I were being tortured.

I couldn't eat. I couldn't think. I couldn't stand myself. The sight in my left eye had been 20–15. Now it was 20–30. I couldn't read. I stumbled around. I tripped over pebbles. All hope had gone.

Those who made it bearable for me were my family—my father and mother, and my two younger brothers, Billy and Richie. They were my support. I believe my dad felt worse about what had happened than I did, but he never let it show.

He told me, "Look, you could have been killed, you could be dead right now. Just be thankful you are alive."

And he was right. When I got to feeling too sorry for myself I thought about all the people who were more unfortunate than I was, who had lost arms or legs, or who were totally blind. And I thought, "What do have to complain about?"

I didn't even enjoy the singing, the entertaining in night clubs. It had been fun before, when I hadn't had to do it, but now it wasn't. It was just something to do.

I tried pitching, working out at the ballpark in the mornings when nobody else was there other than the pitching coach and I. But when I was warned that could make my condition even worse, I had to give that up, too.

That must have been the low spot of my life. I couldn't even go to the ballpark to see my team play. It's not that I didn't want to, but I just couldn't stand it. I went to only one game all summer, and only because the governor was giving me an award.

The award was for courage, but with me it wasn't courage at all. There was nothing I could do about what had happened to me, and I don't think that trying not to feel sorry for yourself is what is meant by courage.

I stayed just three innings at that game. The hardest thing to do without crying was listening to the National Anthem. I went home and moped about the house.

Later that summer, I got the first good news. The doctors told me that my condition had stabilized, and that if I wanted to I could try pitching again.

When I went to the Winter Instructional League in Florida in 1968 I had no hope of doing anything but pitching.

I don't know whether I could have become a pitcher or not. But when I batted I seemed to see the ball well, and I was hitting line drives. Billy Gardner, my manager down there, said, "Look, you're crazy to be pitching. The way you're hitting you ought to go back to right field."

I did that, and I kept hitting until it was time for me to go to my next eye examination in Boston on November 20, 1968. Dr. Charles Regan, who examined me, was amazed.

"You must have been going to church regularly, counting your rosary, because this is a small miracle," he told me. "There's no explanation for what has happened. The hole in your retina has closed. The sight in your left eye is 20–20."

That was the beginning of my comeback, which lasted a couple of seasons. I played well enough [.255, 20 home runs, 82 RBI, in 141 games] to be Comeback Player of the Year in 1969, and despite recurring problems was able to keep going until I finally called it quits.

Baseball is my life, and I thank God for giving me a second chance, a chance I never thought I would get or could have hoped for after what happened in that game in 1967.

ROGER CRAIG

For seven seasons (1955–61), right-hander Roger Craig pitched for one of the finest teams of all time, the Brooklyn-Los Angeles Dodgers. In those glory days he participated in three World Series. Then came the famine with the new-born New York Mets, and Craig suffered through their first two horrendous seasons (1961–62) with records of 10–24 and 5–22. He later managed the San Diego Padres and San Francisco Giants.

There are all kinds of high spots in my major league
career as a pitcher, not the least of which was winning
two World Series games, one for the Brooklyn Dodgers
in 1955, and another for the St. Louis Cardinals in 1964.

And I guess, in a way, a game I won for the New York
Mets in 1953 has to be a standout because it came after
I lost 18 straight to tie a National League record (since
surpassed).

One year I lost five 1–0 games, which tied a big
league record. Another year I pitched four shutouts.

It all adds up to a lot of games to remember, but I
haven't the least doubt about the game I'll never forget,
the one that gave me the greatest satisfaction.

That was the first big league game I ever saw, the
first one I ever pitched and the first one I ever won.

I signed with the Brooklyn Dodgers organization in
1950, and worked my way up so that by 1955 I was
with the top minor league team, the Montreal Royals. I
was having a great season—I think I was 10–2—when
the Dodgers called me up. I was 24.

They were leading the league by something like 12
games in mid-July but they were hard-hit by injuries to
their pitching staff. They needed help, so on the same
day they brought me up from Montreal and Fred
Bessent from St. Paul.

I was with the Royals at Havana, Cuba, which was in
the International League at that time, and was pretty
excited when I flew to Brooklyn.

Bessent and I both arrived at Ebbets Field on Sunday,
July 17.

The Dodgers were playing the Cincinnati Reds in a
doubleheader that afternoon, and both Bessent and I
figured we'd be watching the game from the bullpen. I
was looking forward to it because I'd never even seen
a big league game before.

That was a fine Dodger team, a team of all-stars, with players like Gil Hodges, Carl Furillo, Pee Wee Reese, Jackie Robinson, Duke Snider, Roy Campanella, Carl Erskine, Don Drysdale and all the rest.

The Reds were not exactly patsies, not with hitters like Ted Kluszewski, Gus Bell, Wally Post and a few others.

As I said, I don't think Bessent or me had any idea we'd start when we reported. But Manager Walt Alston quickly set us straight. He told us to be ready because I'd go in the first game and Bessent in the second.

I can't remember how nervous I was, but I'm sure I must have been. But I really hadn't much time to think about it the way Alston sent me out there the day I reported, so maybe that helped.

But the first couple of innings weren't calculated to build up a young pitcher's confidence.

I got the first batter, Johnny Temple, out easily, but the next man, Bob Thurman, drove a line drive into the gap between left fielder Jim Gilliam and center fielder Duke Snider. Gilliam had the best shot at holding it to a single but somehow misplayed it and Thurman wound up at third base with a triple.

A single by Kluszewski drove in Thurman with the first run of the game, but I got out of the inning after that. In the bottom of first, Snider and Hodges hit back-to-back homers to give me a 2–1 lead, but we were still playing "give-away" in the second.

Bobby Adams singled into the hole at short in the second, and Reese, trying to beat him to first with a throw, threw the ball away for an error. That led to another run to tie the game 2–2.

I was beginning to wonder about big league defensive play, but I was too high with the excitement of being in my first game to let it get to me. Besides, my fast ball was moving good and I figured I'd go as hard as I could as long as I could.

As it turned out, it was one of the best games I ever pitched. The Reds got those three hits in the first two innings and none in the next seven.

Of course, it made it a lot easier for me the way the Dodgers hit behind me. Furillo hit a homer in the fourth inning, and Reese hit one in the fifth to give us four for the day.

I struck out six men, walked five, and pitched a three-hitter as I went all the way. What's more, I would have had a shutout if it hadn't been for the mistakes on the field.

But we won 6–2, and that was more than good enough for my first game in the majors.

That's not the end of the story, though. Bessent also made his first big league start, his first appearance, in the nightcap. He held the Reds until the ninth inning, when he got help from Ed Roebuck, and won his game, too, 8–5.

I believe that might be the only time two rookie pitchers ever won a doubleheader as starters in their first big league games, which is another reason I'll never forget it.

Of course, people often remind me of that game when I was with the New York Mets in 1963 that ended my 18–game losing streak. I was 2–20 going into that game, but I wasn't pitching that badly. In fact, some people thought I was pitching well enough to be at least .500, or even better.

But something always seemed to happen, and I'd wind up with another loss.

I finally broke that terrible string against the Chicago Cubs at the Polo Grounds (August 9, 1963). I tried everything, even changing my uniform number from

38 to 13. But the game was tied 3–3 when we went into the bottom of the ninth.

Manager Casey Stengel sent in a pinch hitter for me, and I figured that at least I wouldn't have to take the loss for this one. The pinch hitter, Tim Harkness, walked to load the bases.

Jim Hickman followed with a long flyball to left, and I thought that would end the ninth and send the game into extra innings. I didn't think it had a chance for a homer. But it carried farther than I thought it would to hit the scoreboard for a grand slam.

That gave me a win to end the losing streak, and I felt as if I'd pitched in the World Series. But I had my eye on Hickman as he neared the plate. I wanted to make sure he touched it. I'd have tackled him if he hadn't.

That was a great thrill it its way, but the game that stands out for me is the first one I ever pitched and won for the Dodgers.

JOSE CRUZ

A career batting average of .284 for 19 seasons (1970–88), most of them with the Houston Astros, certifies to Jose Cruz's ability as a hitter. He was a fixture in the Astros outfield from 1975 through 1987, and an All-Star in 1984. He batted over .300 six times, with a high of .318 in 1983 when he led the National League in hits with 189.

Five outs away from the World Series! That's how close it was, the closest I've ever got, and because we didn't make it that one game in the 1980 National League playoffs against the Philadelphia Phillies stands out for me. It was one of the great disappointments of my career.

It wasn't only the World Series, the chance to play in it, that was lost in that fifth game of the playoffs. I had a good chance to be the Most Valuable Player in the league that year, and the MVP of the playoffs if we had won.

It was a good year for me, one of the best I've had. I batted .302 and had 91 runs batted in, played 160 games. You have a year like that, you're doing your job helping your team win.

I've got to say 1980 was the most exciting season I've been with the Houston Astros. All kinds of things happened, things you would never expect. But that's the way this game is. It always surprises you. Just when you think everything is going good, you run into trouble.

Like the end of that season. We had a three-game lead with three games to play in the West Division. Those last three games were all at Los Angeles, and all we've got to do is win one of them. We've got some pretty good pitchers, Nolan Ryan, Joe Niekro, Vern Ruhle, Ken Forsch. You figure you've got to win one game.

But no, we lost all three, all by one run, and ended the regular season in a tie with the Dodgers for first place.

So it comes down to a one-game playoff for the N.L. West Division championship at Los Angeles (October 6, 1980). Luckily, Niekro pitched a great game, and Art Howe had a big day at bat with a two-run homer and four ribbies, and we won 7–1.

We'd been waiting four days to celebrate and we did, but the way things had gone it was more relief than anything else. We'd come so close to losing when it looked like we had it all wrapped up.

All the same, it was a great feeling when we finally knew it was us, not the Dodgers, who had to catch a plane right after the game to get to Philadelphia for the opener of the Championship series the next night. It was the first playoff for most of us, and I was near the dream I had of someday playing in the World Series.

And we got five outs away! That's what hurt the most, when we lost what must have been one of the hardest-played playoff series ever. Two clubs can't be much closer than we and the Phillies were. The last four of those five games went extra innings, that's how close it was.

The first game, they beat us 3–1. I scored one run in the third inning when I got a single and Gary Woods drove me in. But that's all we could get off Steve Carlton, and Greg Luzinski beat us with a two-run homer.

The second game, we scored four runs in the 10th inning to win 7–4. I remember getting a couple of hits in the game and driving in a couple of runs, one of them in the 10th inning.

The third game (Houston, October 10), we won 1–0 in 11 innings. If I remember right, Joe Morgan got a leadoff triple in the 11th, and Denny Walling scored the winning run with a sacrifice fly.

Now we had a 2–1 edge in the series and a chance to win the National League pennant at home with the fourth and fifth game in the Astrodome. All we had to do was win one of the two remaining games. And we couldn't have come loser to doing it than we did.

The fourth game (October 11), that was the craziest one, not that I remember all the details. In the fourth inning, it looked like Philadelphia had hit into a triple play, but the umpire ruled it a doubleplay after a discussion and arguments that lasted for 20 minutes. Not that it made any difference, as it turned out, to the outcome of the game.

What did make a difference was another umpire's decision in the sixth inning by which time we had a 2–0 lead, and it looked like we had just scored our third run off Steve Carlton, who was pitching for the Phillies.

Gary Woods was on third base when Luis Pujols hit a fly ball to the right fielder, Bake McBride. It looked like Woods tagged up at third after the catch, but the umpire ruled he had left the base too early. That cost us a run, which might have made a lot of difference because the Phils scored three runs in the eighth to take a 3–2 lead. We tied the game in the ninth, but they scored two more in the 10th to win 5–3 and tie the series.

There were other strange things in that game, but that ruling on Woods was what really hurt. If we'd had that run we would have gone to the World Series.

But the fifth game (October 12) is the one I'll never forget. That's the one that hurt the most. I don't know how many times the lead changed hands, but everybody was keyed up because this was the one game that would make the season if you won.

I think they led early, then we tied it 2–2, then we took a 5–2 lead and they came back with five runs in the eighth to lead 7–5.

When I recall the five outs we needed I'm talking about the Phillies' eighth inning We were still leading when they had one out in the eighth, but they kept coming, and Manny Trillo hit a two-run triple that gave them a 7–5 lead.

We weren't done, though. We came right back off Tug McGraw, their relief pitcher. With two on and two out, and a run in, I got a single off McGraw to drive in the tying run.

So we went into extra innings for the fourth straight game, tied 7–7. But that's all we could do. The Phils scored a run in the 10th inning, and won it 8–7.

I can't think of a game I've been in that hurt more to lose than that one. That I'll never forget.

LARRY DOBY

The first African-American player in the American League,
outfielder Larry Doby, like Jackie Robinson his predecessor
in the National League, proved to be a standout during his
13–season (1947–1959) career He twice led the American
League in home runs, and in his best all-around season
(1950) batted .326 with 25 home runs and 102 runs batted in.
He also was one of the earliest African-American managers,
for the Chicago White Sox in 1978. He was inducted into the
Hall of Fame in 1996.

People often remind me of the "big brawl" between the Chicago White Sox and New York Yankees in 1957 and ask me how it started.

I was playing for the White Sox, of course, at the time, and we were always going head-to-head with the Yankees. They always won the pennant but we usually gave them a good right in the mid-1950s, especially when Billy Pierce was pitching against Whitey Ford.

There got to be quite a bit of "feeling" between the two clubs. The Yanks had a pitcher named Art Ditmar who had a reputation as a head-hunter. It seemed every time he pitched against us he was putting one under my chin or decking me.

This time, in June '57, we were playing in Comiskey Park. I don't remember the exact situation and the count, but Ditmar aimed one right at my head. When I picked myself out of the dirt, the only thing I could see was Ditmar. He came in to cover the plate when the ball went back to the screen because we had a runner on second who went to third on the pitch.

I warned Ditmar to watch it, he said something to me, and I went after him and landed a good left hook. Right away both benches cleared and there was a helluva brawl. A lot of people remember the picture that came out, with Enos Slaughter of the Yankees, his uniform in shreds, walking off the field with his cap on backward.

But that's not really the game I always think about most. It was just a fight, that's all, and you like to think about more positive accomplishments.

No, if any game would be the one I'd select as the one I'll never forget it would be one of those in the 1948 World Series. That's the one between the Cleveland Indians and the Boston Braves.

I know every ballplayer is thrilled to be playing in a World Series, but I think most people would have to admit it was something even more special for me.

Here I was, a black player, the first to become a regular in the American League, just in my second year with the Indians. The first year, 1947, had been kind of rough, but I'd finally found myself and was doing my share with the club.

It was a special thing for Cleveland, too. They hadn't been in a World Series since 1920. The whole year had been something special, with Bill Veeck putting on baseball's greatest show in Cleveland, drawing more than 2,600,000 fans, and giving it the final touch by signing Satchel Paige.

Everything contributed to this excitement that season. Nobody'll ever forget that we ended the season tied for first with the Boston Red Sox, and it took a one-game playoff—in which Lou Boudreau hit two home runs—to win the pennant for us.

I guess we went into the World Series favored to win it, although Boston had a good club—pitchers like Johnny Sain, Warren Spahn, Red Barrett, and hitters like Tommy Holmes, Bob Elliott, Alvin Dark, and Earl Torgeson.

But we had Boudreau, Kenny Keltner, Joe Gordon, Eddie Robinson, Dale Mitchell, and other good ballplayers, and Bob Feller, Bob Lemon, Gene Bearden, Steve Gromek, plenty of good pitching.

The game I'll never forget was the fourth game. Boston won the opener on their home field, we took the second game, and when the Series moved to Cleveland we won the third one 2–0.

So we were going into the fourth game leading the Series 2–1, with Gromek pitching for us against Sain in Cleveland on Saturday, October 9. If we won this one, we'd be pretty much in command, leading three games to one with Boston having to win three in a row to take the Series.

Still, beating Sain was going to be tough. He'd beaten Feller 1–0 in the opener and allowed just four hits without walking a man.

Boudreau told us to come out swinging at the first pitch if it was close because Sain didn't figure to give us any help by walking anybody.

It worked. Dale Mitchell hit Sain's first pitch of the game, after Gromek had set down Boston in their half of the first, for a single to center. I moved him over to second with an infield grounder, and then Boudreau doubled down the right field line to score Mitchell.

Lou was out trying to stretch the hit into a triple, and got into his second big rhubarb of the series with umpire Bill Stewart.

If you recall, in the opening game Feller and Boudreau worked a pickoff play on Phil Masi, who had taken a long lead off second. Stewart ruled Masi safe, and it got to be the biggest beef of the Series, especially since we lost 1–0.

But just like in the first game, Boudreau lost the argument with Stewart, although once again there were pictures in the newspapers allegedly showing that the umpire had blown the call.

We took the 1–0 lead into the third inning. I wish I could remember the count, but all I recall is seeing the ball clear the 380–foot marker in right-center after I hit it off Sain.

It was the first home run of the Series, and proved the winning run because Marv Ricketts of the Braves hit one off Gromek in the seventh and we won the game 2–1.

Recently, I read a statement by Whitey Herzog (ex-Texas Rangers manager) saying that Boudreau had a guy stealing signs in that game, and they flashed me the pitch Sain threw for the home run.

That's not so. I didn't get a sign. I just hit the ball. Even if I'd had the sign flashed to me, I don't think I would have relied on it.

Besides, as I told some guy who asked me about what Herzog said: "At that time, even if they were stealing signs, they weren't about to give a black player anything. He had to do it on his own."

But that's the memory I prize most. The home run that helped beat Sain in the World Series.

MOE DRABOWSKY

A wicked sense of humor, and a talent for practical jokes made Moe Drabowsky a welcome figure in any clubhouse during a long career (1956–73), in which he pitched for seven teams, serving more than one stint with several of them. At first a starting pitcher with modest success for the Chicago Cubs, he eventually became an outstanding reliever, particularly for the Baltimore Orioles.

My memory seems to profit more from games in which I've suffered than the ones in which I've been successful.

You tend to remember a home run you've given up in the ninth inning to lose a game, or another game in which you threw a wild pitch that hurt. Maybe it's because in a long career there are more of those bad days than there are good ones.

But there were many good games that stick out, too, and I'd have to say that above all the first game of the World Series of 1966, between the Baltimore Orioles and Los Angeles Dodgers, comes to mind as the game I'll never forget.

I'd been on a couple of good teams before I joined the Orioles in 1966, but never on a pennant winner. I had a good year in the bullpen for Baltimore, with a 6–0 record, though Stu Miller and Eddie Watt were our mainstays in relief.

Most people figured at the time the Dodgers with their great pitching had the edge in the Series. But Sandy Koufax had been forced to pitch the last day of the regular season when the Dodgers clinched the pennant and that meant Don Drysdale was their pitcher in the opener, which figured to be a slight break for us.

The Series opened in Los Angeles (October 5), and I remember that morning talking with Frank Robinson, who had come over from the National League to Baltimore that season. He'd had a tremendous year with the Orioles, winning the Triple Crown, and was chosen the American League Most Valuable Player.

Robinson and I discussed the scouting reports, and he had some things to add from having played against the Dodgers for years, which may have helped me that day.

Dave McNally was our starting pitcher, and our hitters gave him a lead but it just wasn't his day.

Frank and Brooks Robinson hit home runs in the first inning off Drysdale to give us a three-run lead, and we got another run in the second.

The Dodgers got one of those runs back in the bottom of the second on a home run by Jim Lefebvre.

Then McNally really ran into trouble in the third inning. He just couldn't get his pitches where he wanted 'em. He walked the bases loaded with one out, and that 4–1 lead didn't look very big anymore.

Later on, I thought it had been a good thing that I got into the first game and got in early before the full impact of being in a World Series and the importance of it hit me. The tension and anxiety didn't have a chance to build up the way it might have if I'd had to sit around two or three games waiting for the call.

But I got into the first game and I got in early, almost before I realized what was at stake.

When the phone in the bullpen rang the Dodgers had the bases loaded with one out and Wes Parker at bat.

I don't know if I was nervous. I know I was concentrating on my job, intent on what I had to do. Parker was a good hitter and could hit a long ball. Any kind of a hit could put the Dodgers back in the game.

I struck him out, swinging.

I might have been a little bit too fine with the next batter, Junior Gilliam, but he was a dangerous hitter in a situation like this. I ran the count to 3 and 2 on him, then lost him. The walk forced in a run, and now it was only 4–2 with the bases still loaded.

John Roseboro, the catcher, was up next. When he hit a high pop-up behind the plate I was praying while watching Andy Etchebarren, our catcher, go after it. I could have kissed Andy for making that catch.

We were out of the third inning, still ahead 4–2, and we scored another run in the fourth for a three-run lead.

Then the strikeouts started coming. Jim Barbieri, Maury Wills and Willie Davis all went down on swinging third strikes in the fourth inning. Then it was Lou Johnson, Tommy Davis and Lefebvre in the fifth.

I had no idea I had struck out six straight batters. I was just concentrating on the mound, trying to make sure I put the ball in the right spots. I was just glad they weren't getting on base, that we still had that lead.

Parker was the Dodgers' lead-off man in the sixth. I got two strikes on him, and Etchebarren wanted me to throw him a fast ball. I shook him off. I wanted to throw him a changeup. I did, and he lifted an easy fly-ball to Curt Blefary in left field.

That ended the string of strikeouts at six. In the following years, Etchebarren would always say to me, "You dummy. You could have had seven strikeouts if you'd thrown my pitch to Parker."

But I was never sorry about that. He did just what I wanted him to do, fly out to left. At that, it was the first fair ball the Dodgers had hit since I'd come into the game.

In the seventh inning, the Dodgers got their only hit off me. Willie Davis sliced a single to left field.

It didn't really worry me. I felt I still had good stuff and my control. We had that three-run lead.

I was able to bear down and get the next three batters out, the same in the eighth, and the first Dodger hitter in the ninth. The next batter was Ron Fairly, pinch-hitting. He went down swinging for the 11th strikeout. Another out and the game was over.

We had won the opener of the World Series 5–2, and we went on to take the Dodgers in four straight, the next three games being shutouts by Jim Palmer, Wally Bunker and McNally. They didn't need any help from the bullpen. My work in the first game was my only appearance.

When the game ended, my only feeling was elation that we'd won. I really hadn't been aware while I was pitching that I'd had anything going. Now it came out.

I'd struck out six batters in a row to set a new World Series record. I'd struck out 11 batters in relief to set another record for a Series. I'd given up just one hit in six and two-thirds innings.

What struck me as especially unusual after thinking about it was that not one of the strikeouts was on a called third strike. Every one of the 11 went down swinging.

I've had occasion to see the films of that game a few times, and I can tell you it's a bigger thrill every time I see it.

Photo courtesy of Los Angeles Dodgers

DON DRYSDALE

Among the most intimidating and competitive pitchers of his time (1956–69), Don Drysdale was the right-handed partner of the Brooklyn-Los Angeles Dodgers great starting duo with left-handed ace Sandy Koufax. Twice a 20–game winner, Drysdale led the National League in strikeouts three times.

People often ask me what was my biggest thrill, or what game of my career was most memorable.

I find those questions a little difficult to answer because—though it may sound corny—I've always thought my biggest thrill to be the day I walked into the Dodger clubhouse for the first time.

That was in Vero Beach (Florida) during the spring of 1955. I wouldn't say I was scared, but I certainly was awed. I'd never been out of California before.

There were all those fellows I'd read about—Duke Snider, Jackie Robinson, Roy Campanella, Pee Wee Reese and Gil Hodges. Pee Wee's locker was next to mine. He was the captain and his number was "1." I got the last number they had left, I think. It was "53" and I kept it all those years afterward.

Those were good years, and I won a lot of games. I got to pitch in five World Series. One of my biggest thrills, of course, was pitching six consecutive shutouts and going 58⅔ innings without giving up a run.

But if I had to choose one single event, one game I'll never forget, it would be the third game of the 1963 World Series against the New York Yankees at Dodger Stadium (October 5, 1963).

First of all, I'd choose that game because I was in the World Series and anytime your team gets into that it's an outstanding experience. Nothing can match playing in the World Series.

Number two, I choose that game because of what happened in the first two games, at Yankee Stadium in New York.

Most of the experts picked the Yankees to win the Series. They had the power—Roger Maris, Mickey Mantle—and the defense, with good pitching. But we had a solid team, too.

The Series opened in New York with Sandy Koufax pitching against Whitey Ford. Sandy couldn't have been much better. He set a [Series] record in that game by striking out 15 men. Bob Gibson broke the record for the St. Louis Cardinals four years later. We won 5–2.

Johnny Podres pitched the second game for us and didn't let the Yankees score until the ninth inning. We won that game 4–1 to take a 2–0 lead in the Series.

An incident before the second game might have helped fire me up for my turn, which was to be in the third game when the Series moved to Los Angeles.

Unlike the National League in which the home team takes the infield first, in the American League the road team gets the first workout.

Before the second game, the one Podres pitched, I was in the outfield shagging flies when the Yankees took the field for their warm-up. On the way in from the outfield I passed Joe Pepitone, the Yankee first baseman.

As I walked past him, Pepitone, either kidding or kidding on the square, said, "For Chrissake's when are you going to pitch? Maybe we'll get a chance to win one."

I retorted, "You'll get your shot in L.A., don't worry."

What he said kind of pumped me up a little more than usual, whether he was kidding or not. Joe's a good guy, a great kidder, but I got kind of fired up.

Besides, after we won the second game, I knew if I could win the third we'd have the Yankees on the ropes. They'd be down 3–0, and would have to win four straight to take the Series, which wasn't likely.

So I was pretty pumped up for the third game. Jim Bouton pitched for the Yanks, and we got a break in the first inning.

Maury Wills opened the game for us with a bunt but was thrown out. Jim Gilliam was walked by Bouton, and moved to second on a wild pitch for our first break.

We got another a moment later. Tommy Davis hit a sharp grounder that took a hop on the second baseman, Bobby Richardson, and caromed off his leg. Gilliam scored on the hit, and we had a 1–0 lead.

I don't remember whether Gilliam told when he came into the dugout, "There's your run. Make it stand up." But that's the way it was. The one run had to do it.

It wasn't easy. I know that.

I guess the Yankees had their best scoring chance in the second inning. Mickey Mantle tried to lay down a bunt and popped the ball over third baseman Gilliam's head for a single. I hit Pepitone, the next batter, on the leg with a pitch.

That put two men on with nobody out, and I was in trouble. I had to bear down. I got a third strike past Elston Howard for the first out. John Blanchard, the next man, grounded out, the runners moving up.

With two out and men on third and second, the next batter was Clete Boyer. I wasn't about to pitch to him with Bouton, the pitcher, coming up next. I walked Boyer and struck out Bouton on three swinging strikes to get out of trouble.

That was the only real jam I got in, but with a 1–0 lead you never feel safe. I remember that Pepitone gave me a scare with two out in the ninth. He hit a ball to deep right, but Ron Fairly backed up and caught it with his back to the wall.

That was the game. I'd beaten the Yankees 1–0. I think they got three singles, and I struck out nine men. We went on to win the Series four straight, Koufax pitching the final game, winning 2–1.

I can think of a lot of highlights in many other games. But that Series shutout, that's the one I'll never forget.

RON FAIRLY

Some might describe Ron Fairly as a journeyman outfielder, but he was obviously more than that because his career extended over 21 seasons (1958–78), and he was a long-time regular on some outstanding Los Angeles Dodgers teams. He played in four World Series with the Dodgers, and went 11–for-29 (.379) in the 1965 confrontation with the Minnesota Twins. Late in his career, he was a fine left-handed pinch hitter.

The greatest enjoyment I get out of baseball—and I love the game—is when my team is in a pennant race, when every game means something extra, when the pressure is on.

This is the way the game should be played, under pressure. Some guys thrive on it, some guys don't, and the stronger ones win.

That's the way it should be, and there's nothing like the feeling you get in the heat of a pennant race when you're straining to do your best and know the other players are feeling the heat of competition like you are.

I remember 1963, when I was with the Dodgers and we built up a solid first place lead by the end of August. Then the St. Louis Cardinals started coming on. They won nine in a row, lost one, then won 10 more in a row for 19 wins in 20 games.

The Cardinals had come up from seven games behind to just one out when we went to St. Louis to play them a three-game series around the middle of September.

Just before the first game, I told Junior Gilliam, "Did you know the Cardinals have won 19 of their last 20?" Gilliam replied, "Is that right? They're really going good."

We beat them the first game, and just before the second game I said to Gilliam, "Did you know the Cardinals have won 19 of their last 21?" Gilliam said, "Is that right? They're really going great."

We beat them the second game, and before the third game I said to Gilliam, "Did you know the Cardinals have won 19 of their last 22?" Gilliam said, "Is that right? That's a remarkable record."

Well, after the third game, when we beat them again, Gilliam said to me, "You know something? I don't think 19 of 23 is such a great record."

That series finished the Cardinals, and we went on to win the pennant and then the World Series, four straight over the New York Yankees.

Those are the kind of things you like to remember, the close pennant races, and we had plenty of those with the Dodgers.

Like 1966. Yes, that would be the one. The game on the last day of the season at Philadelphia. The two games because we had a doubleheader with the Phillies.

We'd lost the first game of the series to the Phils on Friday. Then it rained on Saturday. So we had a doubleheader on Sunday, October 3, and needed to win one game to make sure of the pennant. If we lost both, and San Francisco beat Pittsburgh in a single game they'd force us into a playoff.

Don Drysdale started the first game for us and the Phils had Larry Jackson, a good right-hander, pitching.

It wasn't Drysdale's day. The Phils scored two runs in the first, one on a home run by Johnny Briggs. And they knocked him out in the third inning, though Ron Perranoski came in to relieve and got out of trouble without a run scoring.

Those two runs by the Phils looked like they might stand up the way Jackson was pitching. He was relaxed and throwing hard, and we might have been a little over-anxious, which was understandable.

Naturally, we were watching the scoreboard, and for a while it seemed as if we might clinch the pennant even if we lost. The Pirates were leading the Giants at Pittsburgh in the early innings.

Then in the sixth inning things began to look even better because we finally got to Jackson. He walked Dick Schofield to open the sixth, and Willie Davis followed with a single. I was up next with two runners on and our club trailing 2–0.

In a situation like that you try not to think about what's at stake—in this case a pennant—but concentrate on the pitcher. When you face a veteran pitcher like Jackson you have a pretty good idea what he's likely to do in that kind of a situation.

The count went to two balls and a strike, and I knew Jackson had to come in with one. Another wide pitch and he'd be deep in the hole. He came in with a pitch, all right, a curve.

I got the fat part of the bat on it and out it went, over the right field fence in old Connie Mack Stadium. You can't quite describe the kind of feeling you get from that. A three-run homer to put your club ahead 3–2 in a game that means a pennant.

Only that game didn't win the pennant for us. The Phils scored two runs in the eighth inning to beat us 4–3, Chris Short winning in relief. At the same time, the Giants rallied at Pittsburgh to tie that game 3–3. They were still alive when we started the second game in Philadelphia.

We were in the early innings of the second game when the news came from Pittsburgh. The Giants had won 7–3 in 11 innings. There was no way we could back in now. We had to win.

Sandy Koufax started the second game against Jim Bunning, who was going for his 20th. Short had won his 20th in relief in the first game. But if there was any pitcher you had confidence in it was Koufax. He'd won 26 games, and every time he started you thought, well, he might pitch a no-hitter today.

He didn't do that this time, but he was more than good enough. The Phils didn't score until the ninth, by which time we had six runs. We scored three off Bunning in the third, and got another run in the fourth.

I scored the fifth run in the eighth after a double, and drove in another with a single in the ninth. I had three hits in the second game in addition to a homer in the first.

But it was Koufax's pitching that won the game and the pennant for us. He shut out the Phils until the ninth, and then when they scored three runs with nobody out retired the last three batters to start the celebration.

I won't forget either one of those games of that doubleheader, especially the first in which I hit a home run that almost won a pennant.

TIM FOLI

Players such as Tim Foli are sometimes undervalued, often unsung and seldom noticed as the spear-carriers of the game. But their value is inestimable as the often volatile, always competent shortstop's long career (1970–85), including duty in the daily lineup of the 1979 World Series champion Pittsburgh Pirates, would suggest. And even a .251 career batter can have his big day—or days.

Two games quickly come to mind whenever I think of the highlights of my career and one of them, of course, is in the only World Series I've played in—between the Pirates and the Baltimore Orioles in 1979.

The other game? Well, that's an unusual thing because it gave me a chance to do something unique and you never forget that considering how many thousands of men have played baseball over so many years. I believe I am the only player ever to have hit for the cycle—single, double, triple and home run—in one game that stretched over two days.

It happened when I was playing with the Montreal Expos in 1976 and we went to Chicago for our first series with the Cubs in April. The weather in Chicago that time of year can be bad, and this was one of those days.

The second game of the series is the one I'll never forget (April 21–22, 1976). It was overcast when we started, but it was a lot gloomier for the Cubs than it was for u. We really started hitting. I got a single off Geoff Zahn, the Cubs starter, in the second inning, then a double off the reliever, Tom Dettore.

By the fifth inning we had built up a lead—I forget the exact score at the time—but it was raining, and getting dark. Since Wrigley Field had no lights, if a game was halted by rain it was complete, but if it was called on account of darkness it was suspended and would have to be completed on another date. In this case, since we were scheduled to play the next day in Chicago, it would be completed then before the regular game.

We were already thinking about that when I batted again in the fifth. We wanted to get the inning over with so as to make sure it was a legal game. The Cubs had their third pitcher in there, Paul Reuschel, and I hit a drive to the outfield that normally would have been a double.

Instead of stopping at second base, I kept going, hoping I'd be thrown out at third to end the inning. Instead, I beat the throw to third, so I kept going, heading for home. This time I was out at the plate, which is what I'd wanted, but I had a triple, a double and a single for the game.

We were ahead 11–3 in the sixth when the umpires decided to suspend the game on account of darkness. We gave them an argument that it should have been called on account of rain, but they wouldn't buy it. So the game was to pick up the next day where we had left off.

As it happened, my folks, who live in California, were at the ballpark both games. They were in Chicago for their anniversary. They used to live in Spring Valley, Illinois, and they'd come in to see some relatives, and see a couple of ball games. It turned out they had a more exciting time at the ballpark than they'd figured on.

The next time I batted in that game was in the eighth inning, the second day. A rookie, Ken Crosby, was pitching for the Cubs, and I hit a home run to give me the cycle. The odds against that happening were pretty great. I'm not exactly a home run hitter—in fact, I'd hit only five homers in six seasons at that point of my career.

That was quite a thrill for my folks and myself. To hit for the cycle is tough, but I believe I'm the only guy to do it over two days. So that's a game I'll never forget.

The other one was in the fifth game (October 14, at Pittsburgh) of the 1979 World Series against the Orioles, not just because of what I did but the way the fans in Pittsburgh boosted us though we lost three of the first four games.

We were in sort of a corner, losing three of four. We knew it, but I can honestly say we never felt we were through. We were calm about it. We realized we could climb back, one game at a time, win two, and the Series would be even, 3–3, going into a seventh game. That's just the way it happened. And the fans helped us. They were unbelievable.

I got a walk in the sixth, and Bill Robinson moved me to second with a sacrifice. Dave Parker's single moved me to third, and I scored on a sacrifice fly by Willie Stargell. Then Bill Madlock, with a single, drove in the run that put us ahead 2–1.

It was a real pitcher's game for the first six innings, Mike Flanagan starting for Baltimore, Jim Rooker for us.

The Orioles got a run in the fifth inning and that was the only run of the game until the sixth. That's when we finally got a bit to Flanagan, who really pitched a good game.

We got two more runs in the seventh, this time off Tim Stoddard, who had replaced Flanagan for the Orioles. I hadn't had much luck against Stoddard earlier in the Series, but this time I was able to hit him. Maybe the reason was that I fell behind in the count and I always swing better when I'm protecting the plate.

Anyway, with two out, Phil Garner singled and I followed with a triple to drive him in. Dave Parker scored me with a double to put us ahead 4–1. I'd driven in one and scored two of our runs. I felt like I was swinging the bat better than in any other game of the Series.

Well, a three run lead is pretty good, but you never know against a team as good as Baltimore was. You can't sit back on it. You've got to keep digging. If we lost that game, it was all over.

The eighth inning is what I remember best, mostly because of the crowd. We had a run in and the base loaded when I came to bat again.

As I walked to the plate, the fans started chanting, "Foli, Foli, Foli." It was a great feeling. I had chills.

They don't usually do it for guys who don't hit home runs. We had 50,000 people and they were chanting my name, like they do for the big home run hitters, the base stealers, the 20–game winners. I can't even begin to explain the feeling I had.

Don Stanhouse was pitching for Baltimore. The count went to 2–2. Every pitch the chant was louder and louder. Stanhouse is a good friend of mine and I have films of that moment, and he kind of looked up and made a face like he couldn't believe what was going on.

He threw me a fast ball, and I slapped it up the middle to drive in two more runs and give us a 7–1 lead. I'd scored two runs and batted in three. I'd come through.

But the way the fans responded is what I remember best. What a great feeling it was! That's what makes it a game I'll never forget.

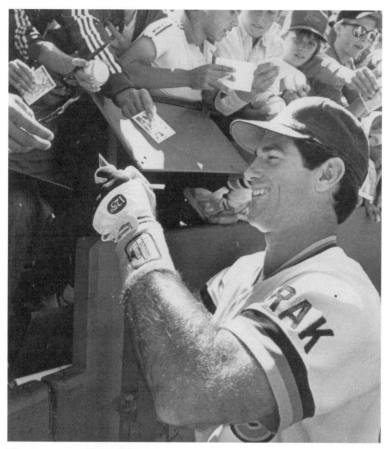

Photo courtesy of *Baseball Digest*

STEVE GARVEY

For the better part of 19 seasons (1969–87) the former batboy was among the outstanding players in the game as a power-hitting first baseman for the Los Angeles Dodgers and San Diego Padres. Garvey reached the 200–hit level in six seasons, and drove in more than 100 runs five times. His career batting average was .294.

There are three of them, really—three memorable
games, each in a different category. All are games I'll
never forget, each for a different reason. One means the
most to me emotionally, another from a team standpoint, and the third as an individual achievement.

I can't imagine ever having a better day as a hitter
than I did in a game against the St. Louis Cardinals in
1977 (August 28) at Dodger Stadium. I went five-for-
five that game—in fact, it was fives all around. I batted
five times, got five hits, scored five runs, drove in five
runs, had five extra base hits, two of them home runs,
three of them doubles. One homer was a grand slam.

The odd thing about that was that I'd been in one of
the worst slumps of my career during most of August.
At one point I had a stretch of 0-for-27, and I didn't get
a run batted in for 21 games.

Then came that five-for-five game.

A day like that has a tendency to make you forget the
hard times that went before it. A slump is annoying, to
be sure. But I just kept telling myself that a lot of better
hitters than I am had slumps, and for longer periods,
too.

You sort of work your way out of a slump. You get a
hit here, another there, and before you know it you're
back hitting again. But I never could have expected to
break out the way I did. That kind of game is a once in
a lifetime thing. I set and tied some records that day.
The five runs scored was a new Dodgers team record.

It started out with a home run into the right-center
field pavilion off Bob Forsch, the Cardinals starter.
Then came the doubles, three of them, and in the seventh inning I hit the grand slam off Clay Carroll, into
the right-center field pavilion, in the exact spot I hit the
homer off Forsch.

A hitter gets a certain feeling in a game like that, a
sort of *deja-vu*, a notion that it's all happened before,

that it's destined to be. You feel that all the pitcher has to do is throw it up there and you're going to get a hit, that you're unstoppable that day.

The feeling builds up with each hit. It's hard to explain. I suppose each hit gives you more confidence—it breeds a sort of confident aggressiveness. You just know you're going to hit the ball hard, and the feeling is even transmitted to the opposition. They almost expect you to get a hit when you're going that well.

That's the way it was that game, which we won 11–0. From an individual standpoint, that's my most memorable game.

I put the concluding championship playoff game of '74 in a different category, that of contribution to the team. That was the pennant-winning game for us, the fourth game of the playoffs with the Pittsburgh Pirates (October 4, 1974, at Los Angeles). We won 12–1, and I was responsible for half the runs.

I hit two homers in that game, drove in four runs, and scored four. I went four-for-five, so it was close to the kind of game I had against St. Louis three years later. But it was a far more important game to the team, and it was especially rewarding to me because it was a contribution to winning the National League pennant for the first time in my career.

In the third category, the emotional one, I put the All-Star Game of 1974 (July 23, at Pittsburgh). Not only the game itself, but the circumstances leading up to it make it a highlight of my career, particularly when it comes to the way I feel about it emotionally.

First of all, I was a write-in selection by the fans as the National League first baseman. That was the first time that ever had happened, which made it all the greater an honor.

Second, five days before the All-Star Game I came down with what at first was diagnosed as a virus. Later

it was discovered that I had the mumps. I couldn't eat
and I couldn't sleep. I was hospitalized, and it looked
like I wouldn't be able to get out of bed, let alone play.

But I made up my mind that no matter how I felt I
would go to Pittsburgh and at least give it a try. There
was no way I could thank the people who had voted
for me unless I went out there and did the best I could.

When I got to Pittsburgh I still wasn't feeling well,
and I had no idea whether I could do much more than
get in the lineup. I hadn't seen a pitch in five days, and
I was hoping to get in some swings in batting practice.
But the weather was bad, and I couldn't even do that.
My jowls were swollen—I looked like a chipmunk.

I talked to Yogi Berra, the National League manager,
and told him I was going to try to play. He said, "Okay,
play a couple of innings, then I'll take you out."

When the game started I still felt terrible. I really had
no idea what I could do. I hadn't had any batting practice, and when I ran a little I felt like I was running in a
dream, sort of floating.

When I came to bat for the first time in the second
inning against Gaylord Perry, who was pitching for the
American League, I was just praying to make contact
with the ball. That's all I hoped for. The first pitch, I
swung and almost fell down. I thought, "Oh no, I can't
even swing." On the next swing I was lucky. I sent a
ground ball up the middle for a single.

The next time at bat, in the fourth, I doubled to drive
in a run. I was beginning to feel better.

Every inning Yogi would come up and ask, "How do
you feel?" I'd tell him that I was all right, so he'd say,
"Well, stay in there a little longer."

In the sixth inning, Yogi used Tony Perez, the only
other first baseman on the team, to pinch hit. When he
came to me after the inning to ask how I felt, I said,

"Well, it really doesn't make any difference. You haven't got another first baseman."

As it turned out, I was the only man to play all nine innings. The sports writers voted me the All-Star MVP, and we won 7–2. I got a couple of hits, and made a couple of good plays in the field. I was happy because I was able to thank the fans for having voted me on the team. In the emotional category, that's the game I'll never forget.

JIM "JUNIOR" GILLIAM

For 14 seasons (1953–66), Junior Gilliam was one of the mainstays of the fine Brooklyn-Los Angeles Dodger teams, and contributed greatly to their winning seven National League championships and four World Series. He displayed his versatility by playing equally well as a regular at second base, third base and in the outfield. He was a pesky switch-hitter who often drew a walk and seldom struck out.

I can tell you about one play of the thousand I made in my big league career of 14 years as a player. One play like that can stick in your mind forever because of its importance and the feeling it gave you to make it.

It was in the 1965 World Series when I came back out of retirement to play third base for the Los Angeles Dodgers against the Minnesota Twins. That Series went down to a seventh game (October 14, 1965) in Metropolitan Stadium in Bloomington (Minnesota) with Sandy Koufax pitching for us against Jim Kaat of the Twins.

We scored two runs in the fourth inning. Lou Johnson hit a home run and the other run came in on a double by Ron Fairly and a single by Wes Parker.

Koufax got into trouble in the fifth. With one out, Frank Quilici doubled to left-center. Koufax then got behind on the count to Rich Rollins and walked him. Zoilo Versalles, the Twins shortstop, was the next batter.

Versalles hit a shot down the third base line. People who saw it told me later it looked like a sure double, which would have tied the game. I didn't have time to think about it. I just dove to my right, backhanded the ball, scrambled to my feet and stepped on third for the force.

That was two out, and Koufax got Joe Nossek to ground out easily to end the inning.

That play saved at least two runs, and maybe the game and the Series because we went on to win 2–0. That's one play I won't ever forget because it meant so much.

But, Good Lord, there are so many games to think about when you play 14 years in the big leagues! And some in the minors, too. When I was playing for Montreal in the International League in 1952, the year before I went up to the Dodgers, there was that doubleheader against Buffalo.

What a day that was! I went eight-for-eight in the doubleheader, and hit a grand slam homer my last time up. Those are the kind of games you don't forget whether they're in the major leagues or in the minors.

Then there's 1953, my first year with the Dodgers. I guess maybe that has to be it because when you're a rookie everything is fresh and new and you're more impressed with everything that's happening.

I don't have to tell anyone about that Dodger team of '53. Just about everybody remembers those names. Gil Hodges, Pee Wee Reese, Roy Campanella, Duke Snider, Jackie Robinson, Carl Furillo, Billy Cox, Carl Erskine, Preacher Roe and the rest.

You can imagine what it was like to be a rookie on a team like that, especially a rookie who went right into the starting lineup. What's more, they moved Robinson to left field to let me play second base. I'd hit .301 at Montreal the year before and they thought I could do the job in the field.

Well, I didn't disgrace myself. I had a good season. Fact is, I was Rookie of the Year in the National League in 1953. I played in 151 games, and I hit .278. So I earned my pay.

We won the pennant easily that year, without much of a race, and went up against the New York Yankees in the World Series. I'd had a good year but I've got to admit I was a little nervous.

Anytime you play in a Series it's something extra, but when you do it the first time, when you're a rookie, you're bound to be awed. The opening game was in Yankee Stadium (September 30, 1953) and just looking around that place, jammed with 70,000 people, was frightening.

I got over my nervousness though and concentrated on the game after the first few pitches were thrown. Allie Reynolds started for the Yankees. Erskine pitched for us.

It wasn't Erskine's day. The Yankees got to him in the first inning for four runs. I remember Billy Martin clearing the bases with a triple.

I'm not sure what I did my first time at bat. I don't think I got a hit. Fact is, I know I didn't.

What I do remember is the second time up against Reynolds. I know it didn't change the outcome of the game but you've got to understand I was a rookie and that made a difference. When you hit a home run in your first Series game that always stays with you.

I can even tell you the pitch I hit the homer on in the fifth inning off Reynolds. It was a fastball, low. Reynolds being a right-hander, I batted left-handed, and I hit it into the seats in right.

I got another hit, a single, in the game to go two-for-five for the day, which was satisfying for a rookie even though the Yankees went on to win the game 9–5, and the Series.

But that home run I'll never forget, and neither will Reynolds.

Two or three years ago we were playing an "old-timers" game and I came to bat against Reynolds. I hit a fastball, low, on a line drive into center field and it rolled all the way to the wall.

Later, Reynolds said, "You always could hit that pitch, couldn't you? Just like the homer in '53."

He remembered that pitch after 20 years! But pitchers are like that. They never forget a pitch a batter hits. It's amazing.

I won't forget that home run either, nor the game even though we didn't win it. It was the first Series game I ever played and I hit a home run. That's something to remember!

TOMMY HENRICH

One of the finest right fielders of his day (1937–42, 1946–50), Tommy Henrich was known as "Old Reliable" on the great New York Yankee teams of the 1930s and 1940s. He rounded out one of the greatest outfields of all time with Joe DiMaggio in center field and Charlie Keller in left. Military service during World War II cost him playing time at the peak of his career.

A lot of people ask me about the third strike that got away from Mickey Owen in the 1941 World Series, or some of the home runs and hits I had over the years. And they mean a lot to me.

Sure, I suppose most people remember that Owen incident better than anything else in my career. We were losing the fourth game of that Series 4–3 to the Brooklyn Dodgers and I would have been the final out when the third strike got away from Owen and I reached first base to start the rally that gave us a 7–4 victory.

One of my biggest thrills, of course, was the home run that won the first game of the 1949 World Series, also against the Dodgers. That was the one that beat Don Newcombe 1–0 when I hit it in the ninth inning to give Allie Reynolds the victory.

That was a big one, of course, and a lot of people like to talk to me about that, just as they do about the dropped third strike.

But seldom does anyone ask me about the last game of the regular season in 1949, something I often think about, and not so much because I also hit a home run in that game.

If you'll remember, 1949 was Casey Stengel's first season as manager of the Yankees, and it was a miracle that we won a pennant we had so many injuries. That's the year Joe DiMaggio didn't play until late June because of the bone spur in his heel.

He came back in a series against the Boston Red Sox and hit four home runs and drove in nine runs to keep us alive in the pennant race. It was a tremendous comeback for Joe after all the trouble he had had with his heel.

The Red Sox had a great team then with Ted Williams, Bobby Doerr, Ellis Kinder, Mel Parnell and a great lineup of hitters. They terrified you, and it was always a wonder that they didn't win the pennant.

It looked like they were going to make it in 1949. But we hung in there right to the end, although it looked like they were in the driver's seat with just two games left. They were a game ahead of us with two games left to play in Yankee Stadium. All they had to do is beat us once.

On the next to last day of the season we beat them 5–4 with Johnny Lindell hitting the deciding home run and Allie Reynolds and Joe Page pitching. It was Joe DiMaggio Day and the ballpark was jammed, and the crowd enjoyed itself because we went into a first-place tie with Boston.

The next day, a Sunday, the last day of the season on October 2, 1949, we were at the end of the line, one game to decide the championship. We had an even bigger crowd than the day before, close to 70,000, and Ellis Kinder was pitching for Boston and Vic Raschi for us. Both were 20–game winners that year.

I had never been able to hit Kinder. He threw a great change-up and I never could time it. When he pitched it was like I didn't have a bat in my hands.

I was thinking about that when the game started and when Phil Rizzuto got a triple for us in our half of the first inning and I came to bat to face Kinder. A man on third and nobody out and I was thinking, "What should I do?"

Joe McCarthy was managing the Red Sox and I could just hear him saying, "I'll give 'em a run. I'm not going to give 'em a base hit." He had the right side of the infield back and I was saying to myself, "I can't hit Kinder. There is no way I can get a hit off him. What am I going to do? I'm not going to hit a flyball."

I finally hit a 14–hopper to the second baseman and that scored Rizzuto with the first run of the game. That stood up until the eighth inning. Raschi was pitching a fine game and Kinder was hanging in there with him. I just couldn't get a hit off him.

When we came to bat in the eighth inning, Kinder was gone and Mel Parnell was in there for the Red Sox. I was the first man up and I was willing to settle for a single or a double. I wasn't going to try and pull the ball.

I fouled off a couple of pitches and the batboy came over to me to say, DiMaggio said, "Go for the long ball, for Pete's sake." So on the next pitch I took a good swing and I hit a home run to put us ahead 2–0.

We got three more runs that inning, Yogi Berra following my home run with a single and Jerry Coleman getting a double with the bases loaded for the big hit. The Red Sox got three runs in the ninth but we won the game, 5–3, and the pennant.

It was a remarkable season for me. I hit a home run Opening Day, a home run in the last game of the season, and a home run in the first game of the World Series.

It's a funny thing, though. People ask me about the biggest hit I ever got and the one that comes up most often is the home run off Newcombe. But I often think about the hit I didn't get because I knew there was no way I could ever get a hit off Kinder.

Yet that 14–hopper to the second baseman that drove in the first run of the game in which we beat the Red Sox for the flag often occurs to me.

It wasn't a hit but it was just as big as one and if you're a thinking ballplayer you have to take some satisfaction in having done what you set out to do.

Photo courtesy of New York Yankees

JIM "CATFISH" HUNTER

Five 20-game winning seasons, a career record of 224–166, and helping to get his teams into six World Series earned Catfish Hunter induction into the Hall of Fame in 1987. His best year might have been 1974 when he was 25–11 with a 2.49 earned run average for the Oakland A's, though he again led the American League in victories the next season when he was 23–14 for the New York Yankees.

When people ask me if it's the best game I ever pitched I have to laugh a little, but I guess it's a good way to start a conversation.

Of course, it's the best game I ever pitched, and I know you can't get better results than that—a perfect game. Maybe some days you have just as good stuff and control and even pitch a shutout, but you can't compare that with retiring 27 batters in a row.

Not that pitching a perfect game or even a no-hitter is something you want to think about pitching some day. All I ever wanted to do in the major leagues was win 20 games in a season and pitch in the World Series and I've done both. I hope to do it again.

But a perfect game? That's just something that happens when you're going right and get a little lucky. Both things happened to me on May 8, 1968, and there is no way that wouldn't be the game I'll never forget.

The strange thing is I never really wanted to be a pitcher. I wanted to be another Mickey Mantle. I played shortstop and pitched a little in high school and played the outfield a little bit. I wasn't too bad a hitter.

I learned a lot about baseball from coach Robert Carter at Pequimans County High School in North Carolina. My four older brothers and I played on a semi-pro team, too. I was an outfielder and one of my brothers, Pete, pitched most of the games.

The Houston Astros sent a scout to watch me when I was a junior. He saw me get four hits one day and told me to work at shortstop and when I was a senior he might come back and sign me.

I turned to pitching full-time my senior year after I'd had a shotgun accident that left my right foot loaded with pellets and blew of the little toe.

I had a 13–1 record my senior year and one of those games was a perfect game and another a no-hitter. I remember pitching three perfect games as a junior, so the one I pitched in the majors was my fifth, although you couldn't exactly compare them.

Mr. Charlie Finley, who owned the Athletics, came out to the family farm to talk to me in 1964 and signed me to a contract. I spent one season in the minors and in 1965 joined the Athletics, then in Kansas City.

I had a lot to learn, of course. I couldn't throw strikes. I was wild all over the place. But Bill Posedel, the pitching coach, finally straightened me out. He taught me how to get my body behind the pitches.

Later on, after I pitched the perfect game, there was some talk that Satch Paige had taught me how to throw a sneaky slider. Satch was with the A's in '65 and told a lot of tall stories. About pitching, though, he never said much. I can't say I learned anything from him.

It took me a couple or three years really to become a pitcher, and I guess it was in '67 that I started to prove myself. I had a pretty good record that year, pitching five shutouts, and although I was 13–17 we were shut out in six of the games I started.

In 1968 I got off to an even better start, and I thought I had been pitching pretty good when I got my turn against the Minnesota Twins on May 8.

I could feel right away warming up that I was going to throw good. I had better control, better breaking stuff, my fast ball moved better than it ever has. No doubt about it, this was my best game.

My breaking stuff at first wasn't as good as it had been in the warm-up but after a while it came around to where it was real good. The fast ball was good the whole game. I went with fast balls and sliders. I threw only three change-ups and one curve ball the whole night.

I might have been pitching a little fine. I ran the count to 3–0 in the second inning on Tony Oliva, but struck him out. They told me later I ran the count to three balls on seven batters. All the same, I thought I had good control.

Dave Boswell was pitching for Minnesota, and he wasn't giving anything up either. We went into the bottom of the seventh with nobody having scored. Rick Monday doubled, and somebody moved him over to third.

I'd had a single earlier in the game but this time Bob Kennedy, our manager, called for a squeeze bunt. I laid it down and Monday scored. I beat the bunt out for a single.

The next inning, the eighth, we loaded the bases.

I was up next and Kennedy, who liked to kid me about my hitting, whispered out loud, "I think I'll pull you now for a pinch hitter." That made me really anxious to hit. I got a double off Ron Perranoski, who'd relieved Boswell, and drove in three runs to make it 4–0.

I wasn't worried about a perfect game going into the ninth. It was like a dream. I was going on like I was in a daze. I never thought about it the whole time. If I'd thought about it I wouldn't have thrown a perfect game—I know I wouldn't have.

There'd been only one tough chance in the game, when our third baseman, Sal Bando, made a good play on Bob Allison's grounder in the fifth. The first two outs in the ninth weren't tough either. But the last one, the one that would give me the perfect game, was hard to get.

Rich Reese was the last batter and I got the count on him to 3–2. Then he fouled off five pitches in a row and I thought he'd be up there all night. But I finally got a slider past him, swinging, for the perfect game.

I couldn't believe it when it was over. I'd pitched a perfect game, driven in all four runs, and to top it off Mr. Finley gave me a $5,000 bonus right on the spot.

Photo courtesy of Minnesota Twins

JIM KAAT

Left-hander Jim Kaat posted one of the longest pitching careers on record (25 seasons, 1959–83), and won 283 games. He was a 20–game winner three times, reaching the zenith of his career with 25–13 in 1966, when he led the American League in wins, starts and complete games. He was noted for his fielding ability, and was selected as pitcher on a Sporting News *All-Star fielding team for 16 consecutive years (1962–77).*

I remember sitting on the bench next to Johnny Sain, our pitching coach with the Minnesota Twins, watching the way Sandy Koufax was throwing in the first inning and marveling at the stuff he had.

I remarked to Sain, "I don't dare give up a run or the game will be over. If he keeps throwing like that we'll be lucky to get a hit. He's awesome."

It was the second game of the 1965 World Series between the Twins and the Los Angeles Dodgers. You could say that the game I pitched in which we clinched the pennant for Minnesota would rank right up there in my mind, but that Series game was slightly a bigger thrill, if you can measure a thing like that.

I guess the Dodgers were favored to win when the Series opened, mostly because they had two great pitchers in Don Drysdale and Sandy Koufax, but we had a good club at Minnesota.

We had some good hitting from Tony Oliva, Harmon Killebrew, Bob Allison, Don Mincher and our shortstop, Zoilo Versalles, who had just a fantastic season and was the American League MVP. Jim "Mudcat" Grant was the biggest winner (21–7) among our pitchers and I was 18–11 that year.

The Series opened on Wednesday (October 6), which happened to coincide with Yom Kippur, the Jewish High Holy Day, which meant Koufax couldn't pitch until the second game, the next day.

Drysdale started the opener against Grant, and we beat Big Don 8–2 to get a good start in the Series.

Our manager, Sam Mele, already had told me I would start the second game and I knew Koufax would be the opposition, which gave me something to think about.

Everybody said he was the greatest pitcher in the game and he had the records to prove it. Just going up against him, let alone in a World Series game, was a big enough thrill and something to awe another pitcher.

Before the game, I didn't even bother to go over the scouting reports on the Dodgers. I figured I knew all about them, so why become confused with a lot of detail. For example, I knew the Dodgers were a low-ball hitting team. I was a low-ball pitcher. That was my strength. If I pitched high, I'd be going with my weakness.

This way it was strength against strength and I figured I had the edge because, on a first-time basis, it's the pitcher who has the advantage, not the hitters. I'd never seen the Dodger hitters before but they'd never seen me either.

Sain always told me, "Rely on your natural stuff and throw strikes. Don't be a defensive pitcher." I went into the game with that thought in mind, although I knew the Dodgers had some fine hitters in Wes Parker, Willie Davis, Ron Fairly and Maury Wills, among others.

I know that pitching against Koufax stimulated me and spurred me on to greater effort, although I tried not to think of him. I tried to train all my concentration on the hitters. But just watching him pitch at the start of the game made me realize why he was the greatest pitcher in baseball.

That knowledge worked for me, though. It relaxed me. Working against a guy like that tended to take some pressure off me. I knew nobody expected me to beat him. That helped.

That Thursday of the second game was a cold, raw afternoon in our ballpark in Bloomington, Minnesota, and I thought that would be to my advantage because I was used to that weather and Koufax wasn't.

The chill and the wet, soggy ground didn't seem to make any difference to Koufax for a long time. He went along inning after inning, striking out one or two men each time. It looked like we weren't going to get to him that day.

As I said, I had the feeling early watching Koufax throw that if I gave up a run it would be all over. But I was keeping the ball low and got into no real trouble until the fifth inning.

With one out, Fairly singled and the next batter, Jim Lefebvre, hit a curving line drive to left field that hooked like it might drop just inside the foul line and go for extra bases.

Allison, our left fielder, was playing Lefebvre quite a way off the line and he had a long run to make even to get near the ball. Nobody thought he had a chance to catch it but he made a tremendous effort, lunged for the ball, caught it, and slid maybe 20 feet after hitting the ground.

It was a great catch, one of the four or five best catches ever made in a World Series game, and I can still see him making it now if I close my eyes.

That catch was definitely the turning point of the game. If Allison hadn't caught the ball, the Dodgers would have scored at least a run and who knows how many more. As it was, we got out of the inning unhurt.

In the sixth inning we got a break when Dodger third baseman Jim Gilliam made an error on Versalles' grounder. Oliva doubled to drive in Versalles and Killebrew's single made it 2–0 for us.

The Dodgers went into the seventh down a couple of runs so they had to pinch hit for Koufax and that was a relief to us getting him out of there. Later, he said he'd pitched a poor game, but he had struck out nine men in six innings so he couldn't have been altogether bad.

The Dodgers got a run off me in the seventh on singles by Fairly and John Roseboro, but I was able to get out of the inning with us still a run ahead.

We got some breathing room by scoring a run in the seventh and two more in the eighth off Ron Perranoski, who relieved Koufax, and we won the game 3–1.

We were up 2–0 in the Series but we couldn't go on to win it although it went seven games.

I started two more games, both times against Koufax, and he nipped me, you could say. He shut us out twice, 2–0 in the final game.

But I did beat him the first time. I faced him and I got just as much thrill out of that game—just going up there against him—as any spectator could watching it.

RALPH KINER

He might have been a merely adequate outfielder, but no one ever is likely to match Ralph Kiner's feats as a slugger. He led the National League in home runs in his first seven (1946–52) seasons in the major leagues, all with the Pittsburgh Pirates. Kiner twice topped the 50 home run level, with 51 in 1947 and 54 in 1949. He later became a respected broadcaster, and was elected to the Hall of Fame in 1975.

I really don't know that it had much to do with what happened but the night before the game I'll never forget I watched some old action movies of Babe Ruth.

It happened in 1948 when I was in my third year with the Pittsburgh Pirates. In early September we were about to open a series with the Chicago Cubs. Wally Westlake and I were invited to the home of Red Ruffing, the old New York Yankees pitcher, who at the time was living in Chicago.

Ruth had died just a few weeks before and naturally we got to talking about him. Ruffing had some old films of the Babe in action and brought them out and showed them on his home projector. It was really something to watch the way Ruth hit the ball.

The next day we opened the series against the Cubs, and it was a big game for us at the time. The Pirates were right in the pennant race that year and in early September we had moved up on the Boston Braves, who'd been leading the league most of the way.

We went into Chicago with a five-game winning streak, and had won 10 of our last 14 games. On September 11, the day of the big game, we were just three games behind the Braves.

We had a good club that year, with Bill Meyer managing us. We had pitchers like Fritz Ostermueller, Rip Sewell and Elmer Riddle. Danny Murtaugh played second, Stan Rojek was at short and Frankie Gustine at third. I played left field and Westlake and Max West were a couple of our other outfielders.

So we were thinking pennant when we went into Chicago. But the morning of the game when I woke up I was sick. I couldn't even eat breakfast. I figured I'd go right out to the ballpark and see if a little workout wouldn't help.

But that didn't help, and the pills the trainer gave me couldn't stop my dysentery. Still, I wanted to play. I didn't miss many games in those days. I told Manager Meyer I'd try it, but he said, "Forget it. You stay in the clubhouse. If we need you for pinch-hitting we'll call you."

I lay down on the trainer's table in the clubhouse. We had the game on the radio and the way it started out didn't make me feel any better. The Cubs scored three runs in the second inning. Fortunately, everybody was hitting that day and going into the sixth inning we were ahead 6–5.

My temperature had gone down by that time and Meyer sent the batboy up to the clubhouse to tell me to get dressed and come out. Meyer figured he might need me to pinch hit in the sixth.

I whipped on my uniform and got downstairs as quick as I could. But the inning was over before Meyer figured on using me. Besides, we scored two runs and were now leading 8–5.

My stomach started bothering me again so I went back to the clubhouse. What I heard on the radio didn't make me feel better. The Cubs scored five runs in their half of the sixth to take a 10–8 lead.

Both teams were scoreless in the seventh and I was back in the dugout when we went to bat in the eighth. We scored a run and had the bases loaded when Meyer turned to me.

"Can you make it, Kiner?" he asked.

"I'm feeling better," I said. "I can give it a swing."

"Good. That's all we need. Just give it your best rip," he said. "Go up and hit for (Mel) Queen."

So I went up to hit for Queen, our pitcher. I was walking on rubber legs and my eyes were watering. I took my time getting into the batter's box, figuring I might gain a little strength. Hank Borowy was pitching for the Cubs.

The first couple of pitches I just stood there and I think Borowy ran the count to 3–2. I'm not sure I took the bat off my shoulder on those five pitches. I didn't feel I had the strength.

The next pitch was mine. A low, outside fastball. I still think I hit it as hard as you can hit a ball. It was a line drive and Roy Smalley, the shortstop, jumped for it. It went right over his glove and kept going. A rising line drive all the way. It just cleared the left-center field brick wall in Wrigley Field for a bases-loaded home run.

I can't remember ever hitting a ball harder than that. A line drive the shortstop thought he had a chance on and yet it went into the bleachers!

That gave us a 13–10 lead but we almost blew it. Finally, we hung on to win the game 13–12 for our sixth in a row. We won the next day, too, but then started to fall behind the Braves. I think the Phillies finally knocked us out.

That was a game I'll never forget because as sick as I was I was able to help out. It's too bad we couldn't have kept going from that point. But Boston had a good club that year and they won it.

I remember I wasn't able to celebrate that pinch-hit home run. Right after the game I went back to the hotel. My temperature was 101° and I was ordered to stay in bed, sip some tea, and get well.

I had a few bid days with the bat in the majors but that one swing was the one that really sticks in my memory.

TONY KUBEK

A neck injury suffered during a touch football game while in the Army curtailed shortstop Tony Kubek's career to nine seasons (1957–65) but they were not without glory. He was American League Rookie of the Year in 1965, and he played in six World Series with the Yankees. After he retired as a player he became a network television baseball broadcaster.

No, I'm not going to talk about the Mazeroski game that wrapped up the 1960 World Series. You can twist my arm but I'm not going to talk about that.

No, the game I remember most also was in the World Series, in my rookie year, 1957. That's the game I certainly won't forget, especially because, among other things, it was the first time my parents saw me play in the major leagues.

It was the third game of the World Series against the Milwaukee Braves and I was playing shortstop, left field, you name it, for the New York Yankees that year.

The Series started out in New York. We won the first game and Lew Burdette beat us in the second game for the Braves to even the Series.

So we were one apiece as we headed by train for Milwaukee from New York, with the third game to be played on Saturday, October 3, 1957, in County Stadium.

We didn't get to Milwaukee without a flap, the kind of furor that always seems to develop on an off day during the World Series so the writers can pep up their stories.

On the way to Milwaukee, we made a stop in a small town about 30 miles away which resulted in headlines all over the country. I don't remember now why the train stopped but whatever the reason it added to the Series interest.

The story got twisted around. Charlie Keller, one of the Yankee coaches, was accused of having said, "This is a bush town. They've got so many cows on the tracks that the trains can't even get through."

Some sources even pinned the crack on Casey Stengel, our manager. But all Casey wanted to do was get off the train and say, "Hi," to the fans who were waiting to see us go through.

Actually, it was neither Casey nor Keller who made a crack about the town being "bush." In fact, the crack had nothing to do with the town itself.

What really happened was that Gus Mauch, our trainer, was impatient because we were delayed on the way to the workout, so he said, "This is bush. Why don't they let us go on and have a workout? I've got to send my equipment out to the Stadium."

Well, Lou Chapman, a writer for *The Milwaukee Sentinel*, grabbed ahold of it and before you knew it the remark got blown all over the front pages in a slightly different version.

That pepped up interest—even if it wasn't needed—for the third game in Milwaukee. Bob Turley started for us and Bob Buhl for the Braves.

I was very nervous, this not only being my rookie year, but also my first major league game ever in Milwaukee, my home town. My parents were in the stands.

First time at bat, as the second man up for the Yankees in the first inning, I hit a home run off Buhl.

I was shaking with excitement as I trotted around the bases and to my amazement there was the most deafening silence I had ever heard. Later, I hit a double to drive in two runs and in the seventh inning I hit another home run, off Bob Trowbridge.

Again, as I went around the bases, I couldn't hear a sound coming from that crowd of more than 45,000 people. It was as if nothing had happened. And the stands were filled with relatives and friends who had known me all my life. Not a peep.

To this day people say to me, "I know you had friends there, but where were they when you needed them?" You never heard them—a deafening silence. People were shocked probably because I wasn't a home run hitter. Or maybe another reason. I don't know what it is.

During the Milwaukee end of the Series we stayed at Brown's Lake, a resort about 30 miles from the city, to have peace and quiet. I didn't stay with my folks. but the day after I hit the home runs—and drove in four runs in the game—a cross was burned on my folks' front lawn.

Even worse, people drove by in their cars and threw garbage at the house. There were phone calls, too: "How can your son be such a traitor to his home town?"

No, I'll never forget that game, not the one in which I hit two home runs and a double.

But nobody'll let me forget the other one, the one in which Bill Mazeroski for Pittsburgh hit a home run in the ninth to beat us in the seventh game of the 1960 World Series.

If you remember, we Yankees led 7–4 going into the Pirates' eighth when Gino Cimoli led off with a single. Bill Virdon then hit a ground ball to me that looked like it would be good for a doubleplay. The ball jumped up and hit me in the throat and I had to leave the game.

That set up the five-run Pirate inning that put them ahead 9–7 when Hal Smith hit a home run. But a lot of people forget that we could have got out of the inning still ahead by two runs if our pitcher, Jim Coates, had covered first base.

We were still ahead 7–5 and the Pirates had runners on second and third when Roberto Clemente hit a ground ball to Moose Skowron at first. For some reason, Coates froze and forgot to cover first. Moose was going to shuffle him the ball but nobody was there.

That would have ended the inning. Instead, a runner scored from third as Clemente beat out the infield hit.

Then came Smith's home run to put Pittsburgh ahead 9–7.

In the ninth, we tied the game 9–9, but then came Maz's home run in their half of the inning.

So it was two plays really, mine and Coates', that lost the game. But mine was the more sensational, of course, me being hit in the throat, so it got the most notice.

No, you're not going to get me to talk too much about the Mazeroski game—the one I'll never forget was the one in 1957 when I hit the two home runs. It wasn't much of a game otherwise as we won 12–3, but it was the greatest for me.

FRANK LANE

Onetime newspaperman and pro football player Frank Lane was one of the most flamboyant front office men in the game's history, and was renowned for his willingness to trade a player at the drop of a bat. "Trader Lane" served as general manager of the Chicago White Sox, St. Louis Cardinals and Cleveland Indians, among other capacities. He even traded managers once, sending Joe Gordon to the Detroit Tigers in exchange for Jimmy Dykes in 1960.

Out of a couple of thousand it really isn't all that difficult for me to pick out the game I'll never forget. The first game that Minnie Minoso played for the Chicago White Sox is the most memorable.

I was general manager of the White Sox then and when I made the deal for Minoso it was the beginning of the Go Go White Sox. That was the big deal and the turning point. I made that deal on April 29, 1951.

I had been chasing Minoso for about two years. My interest started after I saw Minnie play for San Diego, which was a Cleveland farm club at the time. They had Al Smith playing third base and Harry "Suitcase" Simpson was in the outfield, as was Minoso.

Two of them, Smith and Simpson, seemed to be the more complete ballplayers. But Minnie was so exciting that he struck me right away. I wasn't sure whether he was a third baseman or an outfielder.

When I saw him play the outfield I thought he was a third baseman, and when I saw him play third base I was sure he was an outfielder because he had a rather erratic arm.

But he was such an exciting baserunner and such a bear-down guy that I called Paul Richards in Chicago. Richards was managing the White Sox then, and I said, "Now Minoso is not the complete ballplayer that Simpson is, but I like him better than Suitcase. If I get him, where will you put him?"

Richards had managed Seattle in the Pacific Coast League and he knew Minoso. He said, "Well, you get a guy like Minoso that can hit and run like him and I'll find a place to put him."

We were both of the same mind so I went after Minoso. Each spring I'd infest the Cleveland training camp at Tucson, Arizona, always trying to get him but not acting too anxious because Hank Greenberg—who was running the Indians then—was not about to give you at first request what you wanted. He'd rather give you something else.

So I tried to make him believe I wanted Simpson, which opened the way for me to get Minoso. I knew the Indians wanted a left-handed pitcher so I tried to work out something, even if I had to bring another club into it. That's the way it finally worked out, in a three-cornered deal that involved the Philadelphia Athletics.

It took several days to work out the deal. Either Art Ehlers, general manager of the A's, would back out, or Greenberg would hesitate. The Saturday that I closed the deal, Greenberg was out playing tennis in Cleveland. I was desperate to get ahold of him because Minnie had gotten seven hits in a doubleheader playing first base for the Indians at St. Louis.

I was afraid Hank would come back off the tennis courts and learn about Minnie's big day and change his mind. So I called his wife and said, "Clara, I've just got to talk to Hank."

She said, "Well, he's out playing tennis."

"It's very important," I said. "I've got to talk to him before he even takes a shower." I didn't want Hank to get the information from St. Louis that Minnie had gotten the seven hits.

So when he called back I closed the deal over the telephone. It was a three-way deal in which we sent outfielders Gus Zernial and Dave Philley to the A's. Cleveland gave the A's pitcher Sam Zoldak and catcher Ray Murray. The A's sent pitcher Lou Brissie, the left-hander Greenberg wanted, to Cleveland. We got Minoso from the Indians and another outfielder, Paul Lehner, from Philadelphia.

I remember Mrs. Grace Comiskey, who owned the White Sox, saying, "Gee, how can you trade that handsome Zernial?"

Zernial had hit 29 home runs for the Sox, a club record, the year before. I said, "Wait 'til you see the player we got for him."

"He'd better be good," she told me, and later on she subscribed that I might have been right.

Minnie's first game for us was on May 1, a Tuesday, and the New York Yankees were in town. Vic Raschi was the pitcher for the Yankees and we put Lehner and Minoso right in the lineup.

Lehner was the second man up in the first inning and he singled. So Minnie came up for the first time in a White Sox uniform with a man on base. He fouled Raschi's first pitch down the third base line, then belted the next one into the center field bullpen for a home run.

That was the most exciting moment for me because after having chased him for two years he had broken in with such a great slam. He was playing third base, and before the day was over he gave away as many runs as he'd driven in.

Later, as he played more games, we realized he'd be better in left field. The White Sox fans recognized right away what an exciting player he was. He was a good left fielder with a good arm, good speed and a good bat. He was the turning point in our putting together the team.

When I took over the White Sox they were down and out. They lost 101 games in 1949, and I started putting a team together. I got pitcher Billy Pierce for catcher Aaron Robinson, I got Nellie Fox for second, and I had inherited center fielder Jim Busby from the farm system. Then I got Minoso.

All Sox fans know what Minoso became. He was the turning point in making the team the Go Go White Sox, the label the fans picked up as the team became a contender. He started the Sox up the ladder and there were some exciting years ahead.

So without doubt that first day for Minnie is the game I'll never forget. Even if we did lose it.

BOB LEMON

A journeyman third baseman-outfielder at the start of his career, Bob Lemon finished up as a Hall of Fame pitcher with a record of 207–128 in 15 major league seasons (1941–42, 1946–58), all with the Cleveland Indians. He was a 20-game winner seven times, reaching a peak with 23 wins twice. He managed the Kansas City Royals, Chicago White Sox and New York Yankees.

I haven't any kicks coming about anything that has happened to me in baseball, including not being elected to the Hall of Fame right away when I became eligible.

There aren't any "donkeys" going into the Hall of Fame, so it's a great honor just to be mentioned in connection with it, which people have been kind enough to do over the years since I stopped pitching.

The way I look at it, I was fortunate in my baseball career, lucky that it took the turn it did or I wouldn't have enjoyed what success came to me.

Most people know the story of how I started as an infielder, mostly a third baseman. I'm not sure how successful I would've been if I'd stayed in the infield, or even playing in the outfield, which I did on occasion after I came up to the Cleveland Indians in 1946.

Lou Boudreau, who managed the Indians, was given the credit for converting me to a pitcher. He liked the way I threw the ball and gave me a chance to become a relief pitcher in July 1946, just when it looked as if the Indians might send me down to the minors.

I did fairly well that year, winning four and losing five in relief. Following the season, I went barnstorming with Bob Feller's All-Stars and that was a great experience. I learned quite a bit about pitching from Bob, and the next season, 1947, I had a good 11–5 record.

The next year, 1948, was the big one. That was the season we won a pennant and a World Series at Cleveland. Bill Veeck ran the club and we drew over 2,600,000. Boudreau had the sensational year and led the league in hitting and won the Most Valuable Player Award.

That was my first big year as a pitcher, my first 20-game season of seven. I won two World Series games over the Boston Braves, going all the way in the first one.

It was a good year all-around and there were some fine ones after it and, like they say, any time you win it's a great thrill. But the game that was the most exciting to me, even more than the first World Series win, was the no-hitter.

Other guys have said this, so it's nothing new, but you've got to be lucky to pitch a no-hitter. Unless you strike out 27 guys in a row there has to be an element of luck involved in that a pop fly doesn't drop in or a guy beats out a bunt.

For instance, if Dale Mitchell had been a right-handed outfielder I wouldn't have had that no-hitter. If he hadn't been left-handed he wouldn't have been able to catch the ball George Kell hit and it would've dropped in for at least a single. That's what I mean about luck.

We played the Tigers at Detroit before about 50,000 (June 30, 1948) in a night game. Any time you pitched in Briggs Stadium [later renamed Tiger Stadium] with its home run dimensions and came out a winner you'd be happy. It was always a tough park to pitch in, especially for a right-hander like me against the left-handed hitters the Tigers would load up with to take advantage of the short drive to the right field stands.

But I had something extra that night. I had as good stuff as I've ever had. What's just as important, I got wonderful support in the field.

I can't remember the exact innings or plays, not all of them. But I do remember that I was lucky Kell didn't get a couple of hits. I also remember I walked only three men.

I know for sure that if Mitchell, our left fielder, hadn't been a left-handed outfielder Kell would've had a hit. Kell looped a drive down the left field foul line. Mitchell made a long run for it and was just able to reach out with the glove on his right hand and pick it off the grass.

That probably happened about the third inning, and in the fifth or sixth Kell came close to getting a hit again. Only a fine play by our third baseman, Ken Keltner, saved that one. He made a dive for the ball near the bag and was able to get it and make the play.

By the time the ninth inning came along we had a 2–0 lead. We'd scored two unearned runs in the first inning off Art Houtteman, who was pitching for the Tigers. That wasn't much to work with, not in Briggs Stadium.

I knew, of course, that I had a no-hitter going. How could you miss knowing? None of the players would talk to me after the sixth inning. They didn't have to say anything, anyway. I always knew who'd gotten a hit off me and I knew nobody had.

Vic Wertz was the first Detroit batter in the ninth inning, batting for Johnny Lipon. Wertz was a big, tough left-handed hitter, but I was lucky with him. He just tapped one back to me and I threw him out.

The next batter was Eddie Mayo, a pesky hitter with a good eye at the plate. He ran the count up to 2–2, but I got him swinging with a fastball.

That brought up—wouldn't you know it?—Kell, who'd been robbed of two hits. One out away from a no-hitter and here he was again. I got lucky this time and he hit the ball right back to me. I jumped on that ball and, taking my time, threw to Johnny Berardino, the first baseman.

That was it, the no-hitter.

Before I knew it, Boudreau was hugging me and everybody was pounding me on the back and shouting. The fans started to pour out on the field and, with my teammates and the police forming a wedge, I had to almost fight my way to the dugout and into the locker room.

That was my first big thrill in baseball, other than just making it to the big leagues. There were a lot more after that, including the World Series of 1948 and 1954, and those 20–game seasons.

I won 207 games in 13 seasons of pitching with the Indians and yet I'd have to say that the no-hitter was the biggest thrill I ever had. It was the most exciting game of my life and, of course, the luckiest.

After all, if I hadn't been lucky, Mitchell would've been a right-handed outfielder and I wouldn't have gotten the no-hitter.

Photo courtesy of New York Yankees

MICKEY MANTLE

His talent was almost boundless, and despite a game leg Mickey Mantle performed so superbly as to take his place in the pantheon of the greatest New York Yankees players alongside Babe Ruth, Lou Gehrig and Joe DiMaggio. The center fielder's finest of 18 seasons (1951–68) with the Yankees was his Triple Crown Year of 1956 when he led the American League in batting with .353, in home runs with 52, and in runs batted in with 130.

When you look back on the kind of career I had, I guess I could think about a lot of games that might stir up a few memories . . . I know when I read some of the things the sportswriters have written about me it makes me feel it was all worthwhile.

Sure, there are a lot of World Series games out of which to pick the game I'll never forget, especially the one Don Larsen pitched, the perfect game in 1956. Nobody's about to forget a thing like that, not if you live to be a hundred.

But the game I've thought the most about didn't come in the World Series, or in any of the years I was going good. It came in a year when I had most of my troubles, in 1963, when I played just 65 games, the least in any year.

I remember how I thought it was going to be a good year. I had a good spring, and when the season opened I figured it was going to be fine all the way. But right at the start I hurt my rib cage trying to make a throw to double a runner off first. Well, I couldn't swing a bat for a few days, and I didn't know how long it was before I got back in the lineup.

I wasn't in there long, though. I was going good, hitting well and feeling strong, when we got into Baltimore in early June. I remember it was a rainy night, and I chased a ball hit by Brooks Robinson right up to the chain-link fence. The ball went over the fence, but I went right into it. I broke a bone in my left foot and injured my knee.

I can tell you that when they put that cast on my left foot, and I realized I'd be out six weeks, maybe more, I was about as discouraged as I'd ever been. People were writing and talking that I might retire, and I suppose the thought went through my mind that I might as well do it.

I always loved the game, but when my legs weren't hurting it was a lot easier to love. I got as much of a kick out of playing ball late in my career as I did when I first came up—as long as I wasn't injured.

I remember sitting in the Yankee locker room after that injury in Baltimore in 1963 about as down as I could get. I was thinking that every time I was doing well something happens. It had always been like that, and now it had happened again.

I had to use crutches for a while, and somebody asked me, "Do you know how to use those things?" I think I told him, "I've lived with them." And I sure did.

About five weeks after I was hurt, I rejoined the Yankees on a road trip, although I still wasn't ready to play. But Ralph Houk, our manager, wanted me with the team. He told the writers, "Just having Mickey around gives the guys a lift, and I thought it might give him a lift, too. He can't play, but he makes the others play a little harder."

Ralph was always like that with me. Whenever he started bragging about me, it made me believe in myself. I could take the bad days and the boos a little better.

There were quite a few bad days in 1963 until the leg healed. I got tired of sitting on the bench and of hearing people ask when I'd be able to play again. I didn't know.

Two months had gone by since I'd run into the fence in Baltimore, and now we were playing the Orioles again, this time at Yankee Stadium on August 4, 1963. It was a doubleheader, and they won the first game, and they were leading by a run in the ninth inning of the second game.

I don't remember who was supposed to be batting, but Ralph motioned to me to go up and pinch hit. I picked up a bat and started to walk out of the dugout.

That was moment I'll never forget. There were 40,000 people in the stands, and when I came out of the dugout they all stood up and gave me one of the loudest ovations I'd ever heard. It was the first time in my life I ever got goose pimples.

I was scared. Hearing the crowd, I got goose pimples all over me, then I got scared. I prayed I wouldn't look foolish at bat. I was just hoping to pop up or ground out—anything but strike out.

You can't imagine how I felt. I've heard a lot of cheers in my time, and a lot of boos, too. You try to tell yourself the boos don't make any difference, but you hear them all the same. You wouldn't be human if you didn't.

But here they were cheering me—all 40,000 people—just standing there yelling their heads off, and I hadn't done a thing. Just walked out of the dugout with a bat on my shoulder.

I don't remember how I got up to the plate. All I know is I was just hoping I wouldn't disgrace myself, that I'd make some contact with the ball. I don't know whether it was the first swing, the second, or what, but I hit the ball, and it went for a long ride. It went all the way for a long home run, and tied up the game.

I've hit a lot of balls harder, but I can't say that any of them had more behind it than that one. To come off the bench and do that, after the ovation those people had given me—well, I can't express myself well enough to tell you how it felt.

That tied the game, and we went on to win it in the 10th inning, but that wasn't the big thing. It was mostly the way the fans greeted me, and that I was lucky enough to be able to do what I did that makes that one the game I'll never forget.

Photo courtesy of San Francisco Giants

JUAN MARICHAL

Among the outstanding right-handed pitchers of the second half of the 20th century, Juan Marichal would rank near the top. He joined Christy Mathewson and Carl Hubbell in the galaxy of Giants pitching heroes by recording six 20–game winning seasons for San Francisco during his 16–year (1960–75) career, and led the National League in wins with a 25–8 result in 1963 and 26–9 in 1968.

In July 1960, I was supposed to pitch in the Pacific Coast League All-Star Game when Red Davis, our manager at Tacoma, came up to me. He had a funny little smile on his face and he said something, but I did not understand him at first. Finally, it came to me what he was saying.

"Congratulations, Juan, you've been called up by the Giants," Davis said. "You're to leave for San Francisco. Forget about the All-Star Game. The Giants want you to report right away."

Naturally, I was very excited, but not really surprised. I pitched well for Tacoma. I was 11–5 for half a season. I thought maybe I would finish the season at Tacoma but it was not so surprising that the Giants called me up because I was pitching good ball.

Just before I was called up the Giants had fired Bill Rigney as manager, and Tom Sheehan was the new boss. The only thing he told me when I reported to the club in San Francisco on July 10 was that I was going to pitch batting practice for a few days. He told me also to keep an eye on the opposition batters and learn something about them.

Eddie Logan, the clubhouse man, gave me the Number 27 shirt when I reported and I have worn it ever since.

All I did the first week was work out, pitch batting practice, and watch the opposing batters as Sheehan said I should. On July 19 he started me in a night game against the Philadelphia Phillies at Candlestick Park in San Francisco.

I was a little nervous when they announced my name. I felt funny. But as soon as I went to the mound everything was calm.

I did not know the opposing players. Hobie Landrith, who was catching, went over the Phillies hitters with me before the game but we talked about them by (uniform) numbers.

Later on I found out that the first two batters I faced, both of whom struck out, were Bobby Del Greco and Tony Taylor.

Like always, I already had the high kick when I delivered the ball, and I think it was even more difficult for the hitters to pick up the pitches the first time they saw me than later.

I retired the first six men to face me without trouble.

In the second inning, the Giants got a run. Orlando Cepeda hit a double to start it out and Jim Davenport followed with a single to score him. We got another run in the fifth inning on singles by Don Blasingame and Willie Kirkland.

So we were ahead 2–0 by the sixth inning, and the Phillies had yet to get a man on base off me. I retired the side in the sixth and the first man up in the seventh.

I had retired 19 men in a row. Somebody—I don't remember who—made an error for us and the Phillies got their first runner on base.

I got the next two batters out again to retire the side in the seventh.

I wasn't thinking about the no-hitter—as a matter of fact, I didn't even know I was pitching a no-hitter. Honest! Nobody told me about it and all I knew was that we were leading 2–0 in the game.

The Phillies sent up Clay Dalrymple, a catcher, to pinch hit with two men out in the eighth.

Hobie Landrith had told me about Dalrymple. "He's a good fastball hitter," he said, "so don't give him a good fastball to hit."

So the first pitch I threw Dalrymple was a curve ball, low. He lined it to center field for a single.

That was the only hit they got off me in the game. I walked a man later, but I won the game 2–0 and struck out 10 men. I had pitched a one-hitter in my first major league game.

The reporters were all around me after the game in the locker room. Somebody even mentioned Bobo Holloman, a pitcher who had pitched a no-hitter for the St. Louis Browns in his first major league start. I had never heard of him.

I had never even heard of Dalrymple, who had got the only hit off me after 7⅔ innings of no-hit ball. I just knew him by number when he came to bat and by what Landrith had told me about him.

I got to know him better in the seasons after the first one. He never seemed to have too much trouble hitting me. I just couldn't get him out consistently.

That game is the one I will never forget, you know. That first game in the major leagues. Of course, later I did pitch a no-hitter, against Houston in 1963, and that was good, too.

It is a funny thing but that first year at San Francisco I started having back trouble. I spent about a month sleeping on the floor with a bad pain in the back. But I did win six games and lose two.

People started talking about my high kick and how it made it difficult for the batters to see the ball coming off the mound. They thought it must be hard for me to be a good fielder because of the way I delivered the ball. Maybe hitters could bunt on me.

But at the time it was not so easy for batters to bunt. I threw hard to make sure they couldn't.

Nobody bunted on me in that first game. Nobody could bunt what I threw.

I remember Sheehan said after the game, "All right! All right!" That is all he could say. I think so, too, now. It was all right!

Photo by Ron Mrowiec, courtesy of New York Yankees

BILLY MARTIN

One of the most pugnacious, scrappy and colorful figures in baseball history, Billy Martin was frequently in hot water both as a player, and during a long, controversial and often successful career as a manager. He managed five teams, including the New York Yankees for the better part of eight seasons. He also set one of the more unusual major league batting records.

When you start to think about which game really sticks out in your mind as the game you'll never forget, it's only natural that the World Series would be the first thing to pop into your head.

Maybe it could be one of the many World Series games I played with the New York Yankees. Luckily, I never had a bad World Series, and I played in five of them with the Yankees.

In the 1953 Series I had 12 hits, which still stands as a record for a batter in a six-game Series [It has been tied several times since.]

I suppose I could have picked out the sixth game, in which we beat the Brooklyn Dodgers 4–3 to win the Series, as the game that sticks out. That's the game in which the Dodgers scored two runs in the ninth, Carl Furillo hitting a home run to tie it at 3–3.

I came to bat with two on and one out in the bottom half of the ninth, and hit a pitch off Clem Labine to drive in the Series-winning run. You can be sure I'll never forget that.

In thinking about the big game, something else came to mind, too. You know, the first four home runs I ever hit in pro ball were all with the bases loaded. I had 174 runs batted in that year (1947) at Phoenix, and hit .392.

But that was in the minor leagues, so I'd have to say, after giving the matter some thought, that the game I'll never forget would have to be the first one I ever played in the majors, on Opening Day of the 1950 season.

I was lucky in that a lot of good baseball men helped me when I started playing in the minors after I graduated from high school in 1946. Augie Galan, an ex-National Leaguer, encouraged me at the start.

In 1948, Casey Stengel was my manager at Oakland [minor league], where we won the pennant in 1948. After Casey left to manage the Yankees, Charlie Dressen, as smart a baseball man as ever lived, took his job.

I had a good season at Oakland, playing second base and shortstop in 1949, and went to spring training with the Yankees in 1950.

I remember one night during that spring training I was having a beer with Jerry Coleman, the Yankees' regular second baseman. "You're going to get my job," Coleman told me. "I know what you can do, and what you can't do."

I knew I wasn't going to, but Jerry didn't let the thought that I was bother him. He helped me every way he could about playing second base. That's the kind of guy he was.

It was a real good spring training for me. I hit .360, but I knew I wasn't going to make the lineup. Coleman was a tremendous second baseman, and no one figured to take his job that year.

But I was still with the team when the season opened, although I was on the bench for the first game. We opened in Boston (April 18, 1950), and the Red Sox, with Mel Parnell pitching, had a 9–0 lead in the sixth inning.

Allie Reynolds started for the Yankees, and the Red Sox got three runs off him in the first inning. They scored another run in the second, and five more in the fourth.

We got four runs in the sixth inning, when Stengel sent in Dick Wakefield to bat for Coleman. I went in to play second base in Coleman's place.

The Red Sox picked up another run in the seventh, and had a 10–4 lead when I came to bat for the first time in the majors in the eighth.

I guess Stengel figured the game was over because he let me bat although there were two men on when I came up.

Parnell was still pitching, and I hit a double off the top of the left field wall to drive in a run.

We just kept going from there, and I got to bat again the same inning with the bases loaded. This time I hit a single to left, and drove in two more runs, off Walt Masterson, who had relieved for Parnell.

It was an unbelievable inning. We hit everything in sight, and the Red Sox used five pitchers. We sent 14 guys to the plate and eight of them got base hits. I remember Joe DiMaggio getting a big double.

We scored nine runs that inning to take a 13–10 lead, and got a couple of more runs in the ninth to win 15–10.

It's hard to believe that with all that hitting, and with all those great hitters, like DiMaggio, Ted Williams, Bobby Doerr and Yogi Berra, that only one home run was hit in the game. That was hit by Billy Goodman, who never hit too many.

After the game, I remember all the reporters gathering around DiMaggio, talking to him about the unbelievable rally. Joe said to 'em, "Think I'm doing good?—how about that little Dago," and pointed to me. That's the kind of guy DiMaggio was.

Those two hits didn't earn me a job. The next day Coleman was back at second base, and it wasn't long before the Yankees sent me to Kansas City [then a minor league team]. But I came back before the season ended.

That's the game I'll never forget, the first game I ever played in the majors, and in which I'd had two hits in the same inning.

That's in the record book: most hits in one inning in first major league game.

Photo courtesy of Montreal Expos

GENE MAUCH

A light-hitting utility infielder during his playing days (1944–57), Gene Mauch won wide respect as a resourceful manager who got the most out of the available talent. He managed four major league teams for a total of 26 seasons between 1960 and 1987, but never was able to lead his club into a World Series. His greatest misfortune came in 1964 when his Philadelphia Phillies "blew" a commanding lead late in the season.

There were many games that were unusual in some way when I was a player but they didn't have the significance they had when I was managing in the big leagues.

One game I suppose I could have chosen as the game I'll never forget would be the no-hitter Jim Bunning pitched against the New York Mets in 1964 when I was managing the Philadelphia Phillies. That was a great game, but again it didn't have the significance that some other games had.

Besides we won that game, and to me the games that you lose stick with you longer. Those are the games in which something went wrong and you didn't do the kind of job you should have.

Thinking about it, the game that I'd have to choose as the one that sticks is one in the 1964 season when we had that 10–game losing streak at the end. That's when we had a 6½ game led with 12 games left to play and then didn't win the pennant.

The first game of that 10–game streak isn't the one I'm thinking of, but I haven't forgotten that one either. That's a game in which we were playing Cincinnati at Philadelphia and we had Art Mahaffey pitching. The Reds had John Tsitouris and they went along for five innings without anybody scoring.

Chico Ruiz singled for the Reds in the sixth and I can't remember how he got over to third base. But he was over there with Frank Robinson at bat when he took off for home. He stole home and the run beat us 1–0 and that was the first game of the 10 we lost in a row.

That reminds me that just two days before the Los Angeles Dodgers beat us almost the same way. Willie Davis stole home to beat us 4–3.

We won a game in between and the steal of home by Ruiz came in the first game of our 10–game string. The second game we lost to the Reds when Frank Robinson hit a two-run homer, and we lost again to the Reds the third day.

But the game I'll never forget was the fifth game of that losing streak (Friday, September 26, 1964) in old Connie Mack Stadium at Philadelphia. We were playing the Milwaukee Braves and now—after losing four in a row—we were down to 2½ games ahead of Cincinnati, in second place.

It shows you how quickly a lead can shrink. We had been going good. Bunning, whom we'd gotten from Detroit the previous winter, was a big help (he was 19–8 that year), and the kids like Richie Allen and Johnny Callison were having great years. That was Allen's first year and he was just great for us.

Anyway, I can't remember who was pitching in that game, but we'd lost four in a row and it didn't look too good when the Braves had a 3–1 lead going into the eighth inning. But Allen and Callison put on a great display of determination and desire to win which I'll never forget.

There was one down in the bottom of the eighth when Allen singled off Billy Hoeft, who was the second pitcher for Milwaukee. That's when Callison hit a home run to tie the game 3–3, and that gave me a lift to see the way the kids kept battling back.

Both clubs went scoreless in the ninth, and we went into the 10th inning tied 3–3. That's when the Braves really hurt us. They scored twice and you know how big two runs look when you're in extra innings.

They got their two runs when Ty Cline singled and Joe Torre followed with a home run. That put us behind 5–3 going into the bottom of the tenth and it looked like we were going to lose our fifth in a row right there.

But we weren't through. We had one out in the 10th when Cookie Rojas singled and Allen came to bat again. Well, he hit the ball—you know how high that wall was in right-center in Philly—and the ball hit the center field fence and bounced away from the Braves outfielders. It rolled around out there, and after Rojas scored Allen came all the way around for an inside-the-park homer to tie the game 5–5.

It was a great effort, and it was ironic that we lost the game on a bloop hit. Gary Kolb started it out for the Braves in the 12th inning with an infield hit and Gene Oliver walked. Then Eddie Mathews singled off our third baseman's glove—it was Frank Thomas—to score Kolb with the first run.

Oliver had gone to third on the play and when Mathews was out going to second, he broke for the plate. Our second baseman Tony Taylor's throw got away from catcher Clay Dalrymple and Oliver scored the second run to make it 7–5.

And that's the way the game ended, 7–5, our fifth loss in that string of 10.

What makes that game stick out in my mind is that it was so indicative of how hard our club played. It was scrambling, fighting, clawing to win, but it couldn't.

The game didn't represent anything special at the time except how hard those kids were trying to win the pennant. As time went on, it seemed such a shame we couldn't capitalize on the way our kids were playing. We kept losing and you know what happened—St. Louis won the pennant.

But we didn't lose because we gave up. Those kids tried every game, every day, and I can't think of a game that shows more just how hard they tried.

That's the game I'll never forget!—one we lost.

To me, the only games that stick with you are the ones you lose. The ones you win you did everything right—they don't teach you anything.

Photo by Ray De Aragon

WILLIE MAYS

Branch Rickey, the front office "genius" most remembered for opening up baseball to African Americans by giving Jackie Robinson his opportunity, considered Willie Mays the perfect player. He wrote: "Willie Mays' true greatness is his equal strength hitting, running and throwing, and the intensity with which he executes every play." Those talents made Mays the game's finest player for almost his entire career (1951–73), virtually all as a New York-San Francisco Giant.

People suppose, maybe because there's been so much talk about it, and they've shown it so much on TV, that my greatest thrill was the time I made that catch on Vic Wertz in the 1954 World Series.

I'm not saying it wasn't a great thrill because it was—so was winning that World Series with the New York Giants over the Cleveland Indians. There have been a lot of other big thrills for me in playing baseball, as most people know, seeing I was lucky enough to be out there so long, and with such good teams.

Heck, what more of a thrill can there be than seeing Bobby Thomson hit that home run in the playoffs against the Brooklyn Dodgers in 1951 to win the pennant for us? I was in the on-deck circle waiting my turn at bat when he did it.

But no matter what game or play people remind me of, asking me if it was my biggest thrill, I always tell 'em, "Well, if you're talking about the game in which I hit four home runs, that's the one."

Sure, all the other things mean a lot to me, but my biggest day, the one I'll never forget, that's the four-home run game.

It happened in Milwaukee on April 30, 1961, a Sunday, and it was the wildest game I ever was in for home runs. We Giants hit eight home runs in that game, and the Braves had a couple, Hank Aaron hitting both of them.

So that's 10 home runs in a game, and you're not going to see that more than once or twice in a lifetime. I know I haven't, and I haven't done anything like that four-home run game before or since. The greatest day of my baseball career, I call it.

More than how I hit four home runs that day, what I remember is the things that happened before the game, in fact the couple of days before.

I wasn't hitting at all when we got to Milwaukee. I was in a slump, and I thought it was getting deeper. Not only hadn't I had a hit the two days before, but I didn't hit one ball good at all.

The funny thing is that my team was hitting real good. The Giants got 15 hits Saturday, five of them home runs, and I didn't get good wood on a ball once.

I don't say I was feeling bad about the way I was going. I hadn't had any hits the first game, Friday, either, so I was 0–for-7 in the series. But I was thinking what to do to get out of what some people might call a slump.

Saturday night I had a chance to talk it over with Leo Durocher [the former Giants manager] and he suggested a few things I might be doing wrong—gripping my bat, my stance and so on. That made me feel a little better. Leo, who wasn't with the Giants then, always could help me, and I figured, well, things will pick up.

Then I got sick. I was rooming with Willie McCovey at the time, and he brought a double order of spare ribs into the room. They tasted good, but an hour later I felt like somebody had kicked me in the stomach.

I was so sick I had McCovey call the trainer up to the room, and he gave me some medicine to settle my stomach. After a while I felt better and fell asleep.

In the morning, I wasn't sure I'd be able to play that day. I felt weak as a cat. I figured, well, I'll see how I am before the game and decide. I can try and play.

Batting practice wasn't too bad. I could get the bat around even if I didn't feel real strong. You never can tell, I thought, "I might just get four hits today."

Lew Burdette, a right-hander, was pitching for the Braves [then in Milwaukee before moving to Atlanta]. But I could always hit right-handers so that didn't bother me. We had Billy Loes pitching, and he never had an easier day. We won 14–4.

Now I can't remember what happened on every pitch that day. All I remember is that I hit the ball good every time I got wood on it.

In the first inning, I hit a home run to left center. They say it went 420 feet. Nobody was on base.

In the second inning, there were two men on, and this time I hit a pitch by Burdette some 400 feet again, into the right field stands.

The next time up Burdette was gone and Seth Morehead was pitching in the fourth inning. There was a man on, and I hit the ball to straightaway center. They say it went 450 feet.

I think up to that time I'd hit only one ball harder in my life. That was in old Sportsman's Park in St. Louis.

Three-for-three. Three home runs, and when I came to bat again in the fifth inning I think some of the Milwaukee fans were pulling for me to hit that fourth straight.

I didn't do it. Moe Drabowsky was pitching for Milwaukee now and I hit the ball good, but right at the center fielder Aaron. It was hit good, but nowhere near to going out of the park.

I got the fourth home run in the eighth inning with a man on, and it was hit almost as far as the third one. This one was off Don McMahon, who later pitched for the Giants, and they say it went 430 feet.

Four home runs and eight runs batted in. I almost had a chance to make it more. The crowd was cheering for me to get another chance to bat in the ninth. I was in the on-deck circle with two out, but Jim Davenport grounded out so I didn't get to try for the fifth home run.

I was just up there swinging. The pitches were in there, and I just connected. What more can you say about my four-home run day?

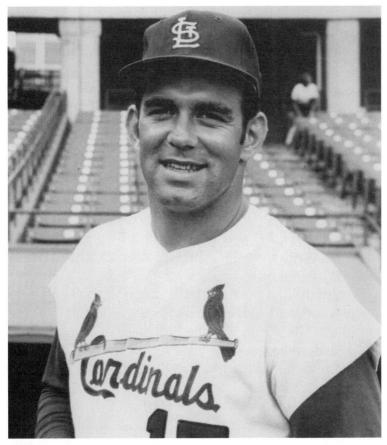

Photo courtesy of St. Louis Cardinals

TIM McCARVER

Bob Gibson and Steve Carlton were among the Hall of Fame pitchers Tim McCarver caught during a long career (1959–1980) behind the plate, most of it with the St. Louis Cardinals and Philadelphia Phillies. McCarver's best year as a hitter was 1967 when he batted .295 with 14 home runs and 69 runs batted in for the World Series champion Cardinals. McCarver later became a notable television commentator.

There's not the least doubt in my mind which game I consider the most memorable of my career, though I played in three World Series with the St. Louis Cardinals and we won two of them.

I was only 22 in 1964 and it was my second full season in the big leagues. I've played a lot of years since, but I don't think there's ever been a season more exciting, or more surprising than that one.

Johnny Keane was the Cardinals manager that year and we had a good team, but we didn't figure to win it. We had Bill White at first base, Dick Groat at shortstop, Curt Flood in center, Ken Boyer at third, Mike Shannon in right, and among the pitchers were Bob Gibson, Ray Sadecki, Curt Simmons and Barney Schultz.

We got off to a poor start, playing only .500 ball until mid-season and it looked like we wouldn't be in the running. The Philadelphia Phillies, Cincinnati Reds and San Francisco Giants were fighting it out. The Phils looked like the best bet to win the pennant.

It's always hard to pin down the turning point of the season, but it probably came on June 15, the trading deadline. Bing Devine made a deal with the Cubs they're still talking about in Chicago. You can't blame the Chicago fans because the Cardinals got Lou Brock in the trade.

At the time, it didn't seem like such a good deal for St. Louis. Devine sent pitcher Ernie Broglio, who'd been a big winner for us, with a couple of other pitchers to the Cubs for Brock and two other players. A lot of people thought we gave up too much because our pitching wasn't all that strong, for Brock, who wasn't hitting with the Cubs.

The change of scenery did wonders for Brock. Almost from the moment he came to us he started hitting and running. He hit over .300 for the rest of the season. He started stealing bases, taking the extra base, making things happen with his speed, and hitting home runs. He gave us a lift.

Slowly, we began to move, gaining on the Phillies, who were comfortably in first place. We were 11½ games out on August 23, then only six games out on September 9 when we went to Philadelphia for a two-game series. If we won them both, we'd be only four out. But we split the seat and the Phils still had a six-game lead.

A few days later, the Phils still had a 6½–game lead with 12 games to play, and it looked like the best we could do was settle for second place money. Nobody could have imagined what was about to happen. Who would have supposed that the Phils could lose 10 straight at that point?

But they did go into an unbelievable slump and first Cincinnati then we went past them into first place. We went down to the last day of the season when it could have been in effect a three-way tie for the pennant. In fact, the Giants were eliminated only the day before. But we beat the New York Mets the last day while the Phillies beat Cincinnati so we won the pennant.

So there we were, somewhat to our surprise, in the World Series against the New York Yankees. (This was before the institution of divisional play, etc.).

As I said earlier, I was only 22 at the time, and excited about playing in my first Series. Not that you ever get over regarding the Series as something special. I had much the same feeling in '67 and '68, the other two years in which we won pennants in St. Louis. But the first one, naturally, is the most exciting.

I'm sure the Yankees were favored to beat us. They had Mickey Mantle, Roger Maris, Elston Howard and the rest of an outstanding group of players, and pitchers like Whitey Ford and Mel Stottlemyre.

We beat the Yankees in the opener, but what really hurt the Yankees was that Ford came up with arm trouble and was unable to pitch in the rest of the Series.

Each club won two of the first four games, which brings us to the game I'll never forget, the fifth game (Monday, October 12, 1964, in Yankee Stadium).

Gibson started for us. He'd pitched the second game and struck out six men in the first three innings, but the Yankees had come on to beat him. Stottlemyre started for the Yanks. He'd won the second game.

Gibson seldom had better stuff than he had in that fifth game. He struck out 13 men. Stottlemyre also pitched well. We couldn't do anything with him until the fifth inning when we scored a pair of runs.

That looked like it might be enough. Gibson was particularly effective in the shadows at Yankee Stadium. He also was crossing up the scouting reports the Yankees were relying on. They said he threw mostly fastballs. In this game, he threw probably 30 percent breaking balls, which were down.

So we went into the bottom of the ninth leading 2–0. The Yankees got a break when Mantle hit a grounder to Groat, who charged it but couldn't handle it. Gibson struck out Howard, then made a great play on Joe Pepitone that probably saved the game.

Pepitone hit a line drive that Gibson deflected to the left of the mound. Gibson shot off the mound to his right, grabbed the ball, turned and threw out Pepitone by inches. Had Gibson not made that play, in effect the Yankees would have won the game 3–2 because the next batter, Tommy Tresh, hit a home run into the right-center field stands. That tied the game 2–2.

So we went into extra innings.

Pete Mikkelsen was pitching the 10th for the Yanks, and he walked White to lead off the inning. Boyer laid down a bunt intending to sacrifice White to second, but beat out the play. With two men on, Groat hit into a force play on Boyer.

I was up with men on third and first and one out. I wanted to avoid hitting into a doubleplay and get one in the air hoping to hit it deep enough for a sacrifice fly to score the lead run. I got the pitch I was looking for, a fastball. I got it all, a home run into the right field stands with two men on.

We won the game 5–2 and though the Yankees won the next one, we went on to win the Series.

I had a good Series, getting at least one hit in every game. I went 11-for-23, a .478 average. But the game that stands out for me was the fifth, the one in which I hit a three-run homer in the 10th. That's the game I'll never forget.

JOHNNY MIZE

There's no doubt first baseman Johnny Mize was among the most formidable hitters of his time (1936–42, 1946–53). He could hit for average (.312 career, leading the National League in batting with .349 in 1939), power (leading in home runs four times), and was difficult to strike out. In 1947 he hit a career-high 51 home runs and struck out only 42 times for the New York Giants. He was inducted into the Hall of Fame in 1981.

Not long ago I was at an old timers' game in New York and Mel Allen, the old broadcaster who was going to announce each player as he came up to hit, came over to me. He liked to say something special about each old-timer coming to bat.

"John, what can I say about you?" Mel asked me.

I said, "Mel, I've been going off and on to old timers' games for years and nobody's ever mentioned that I hold the record for most home runs ever hit by a left-handed hitter in a single season in the National League."

"Is that right?" Mel said. "I didn't know that. Let me look in the record book to make sure."

Now that's the way it is. Here's Allen, a man who has been in baseball for many years, and he didn't know about my record. He got the book out and he looked, then said, "John, you're right. Everyone else who's hit 51 or more home runs in the National League is a right-handed hitter. You're the only left-handed hitter who has done it."

Allen called over Joe DiMaggio and Mickey Mantle, who were standing nearby, and told them about the record. They said, "You're all wet, Mel." He said, "If you don't believe it, look it up in the book." So they did and they were as surprised as Mel was.

But it's a fact. The 51 homers I hit in 1947 are still a National League record for a left-handed batter. I've never seen anybody write about or mention it.

I was in the big leagues from 1936 to 1953, which would have been 18 seasons if I hadn't been in the armed services during World War II for three years. I played for three teams, the St. Louis Cardinals, New York Giants and New York Yankees.

My best years as a player were probably with the Cardinals and the Giants, but my most memorable games came with the Yankees because all five years I was with them we won the World Series.

I guess people think of me as a pinch hitter with the Yankees, but I played some first base, too. Casey Stengel, the manager, used me an awful lot against left-handed pitchers and would play Joe Collins, a left-handed batter like myself, against right-handed pitchers.

It was sort of unusual, but Casey knew I could hit left-handers as well as I did right-handers.

I never found pinch-hitting hard. Like any time you went to bat they had to get the ball over the plate to you. The only trouble was that with the Yankees you didn't go up there every day. With a losing club you are up there quite often, but with a winning club you may not go to bat more than once every three or four days.

I made the best of it, though. I studied what I was doing. I knew pretty well when Casey was about to call on me. When the other team was hitting and we were in the field I used to go into the clubhouse, take my bat out of the locker where I kept it, and start swinging. One time I was in the clubhouse and was swinging like I was hitting a golf ball.

The clubhouse attendant noticed what I was doing and he said, "John, you don't swing like that, do you?"

I said, "Yeah, but I've been watching the way Mike Garcia (Cleveland Indians) is pitching today and he looks like he's pitching everybody low and inside. So it looks like I'll have to golf one."

Next inning, Casey sends me up to pinch-hit—he never said much of anything other than "Go up and hit"—and the first pitch Garcia threw me was low and inside and darned if I didn't hit it into the right field bleachers.

The clubhouse boy was the first to greet me when I crossed the plate and he said, "Well, you had that one figured right."

I can't really pinpoint a single game that would be my most memorable, the one I'd never forget, because there were several of them, especially during the five years (1949–53) we won the World Series with the Yankees.

There was that '49 Series against the Brooklyn Dodgers. Each team won a game 1–0, Allie Reynolds beating Don Newcombe in the opener, then Preacher Roe beating us in the second game. I guess you might say the third game was the key and I drove in two runs with a pinch-hit single with the bases loaded in the ninth to help us win 4–3. We went on to take the Series in five games.

But I guess, if I think about it, the game I'll never forget came in the '52 Series, again against the Dodgers. Though we won the Series, we didn't win that game, but it is still a great memory for me.

The game I'm talking about was the fifth game, played on a Sunday (October 3, 1952, at Yankee Stadium). Each team had won two games up to that point and I was having a good Series. I hit a home run pinch-hitting in Friday's game, though we'd lost it. Then I hit a home run Saturday off Joe Black, the first run for us in a game we won 2–0.

The Sunday game, the one I remember best, Carl Erskine was pitching for the Dodgers, and Casey had me playing first base. Brooklyn scored a run early, then three more in the fifth inning when Duke Snider hit a homer, to take a 4–0 lead.

We got to Erskine in the fifth, scoring five runs. I drove in the first three with a home run into the right field bleachers, my third in three games. The Dodgers came back, though, and the game went into extra innings. The Dodgers finally got a run in the top of the 11th inning.

Erskine was still pitching when I came to bat in the bottom of the 11th. He'd retired 15 or 16 batters in a row at that point. But I hit one well and I thought it was going to be another homer to tie the game. But the guy in right field, Carl Furillo, ran out, put his hand against the wall to use it as a springboard, and jumped high enough to catch the ball.

We lost the game to trail 3–2 in the Series, but won the final two to beat the Dodgers again for our fourth World Series in a row and the next year we made it five.

There are a lot of great days to remember about those years with the Yankees and even if it may seem odd I guess the day I just missed getting four home runs in three World Series games was the most memorable for me.

LINDSEY NELSON

For many years Lindsey Nelson was the voice of the New York Giants and then the Mets after they began play in the National League in 1962. He broadcast games both on WOR-TV and radio station WJRZ on the East Coast. He also was a nationally-known broadcaster, especially during the years when he handled the baseball Game of the Week for a major television network.

A funny thing, though, I don't remember the details of as many games as you would think I would. I make almost a conscious effort to block out most of them so as to start the next game fresh. But naturally there are some that stick out, like the day Willie Mays hit four home runs in a game, and the time Jim Bunning pitched his perfect game.

When I think about it, that (the Bunning game) would have to be the one. There were a lot of things that went together to make that game outstanding, naturally the fact that Bunning set down 27 men in order being the most important, but other things, too.

Like it was Father's Day, and it was the first day of summer, June 21, 1964. It was also the first year Shea Stadium was open. There was a big crowd on hand because it was a Sunday and a holiday and the Phillies and Mets provide a good rivalry since the cities are only 90 miles apart.

Bunning was the starting pitcher for the Phillies in the first game of the doubleheader against Tracy Stallard of the Mets. It was Bunning's first year in the National League. He'd had a good career with the Detroit Tigers in the American League and had pitched a no-hitter for them against the Boston Red Sox, then had been traded to the Phils.

You always figured Bunning for a good game, especially on a day when he had the good curve ball, which was tough for anybody to hit, coming as it did from the side-arm. He started out this particular day, as Bunning always did, getting the side out 1–2–3, which was nothing unusual.

While Bunning was mowing them down, Stallard wasn't having as much luck, the Phils scoring single runs in both the first and second innings. In the fifth for the Mets, Joe Christopher led off by popping out to shortstop Cookie Rojas.

The next man up was Jesse Gonder, the catcher. He was a pretty good left-handed hitter and he ripped a line drive out toward right that looked like a hit when it left the bat. But second baseman Tony Taylor left his feet in diving for the ball, got a glove on it to knock it down, and threw out Gonder at first.

As it turned out later, that was the only tough fielding play of the game. But you weren't thinking of that yet, certainly not in the fifth inning. Well, the Phils got four more runs in the sixth so they had a 6–0 lead going into the Mets' half of the inning.

Now this is about the time you notice that nobody has been on base yet and yet you're not really thinking about a perfect game. You figure that'll be over with pretty soon because there hasn't been one in the National League for 84 years (since 1880).

Yet here is Bunning rolling along and as you get to the seventh inning you start to wonder about it. As a broadcaster, it gives you something to think about because many of them have this thing about whether or not to mention on the air when a man is pitching a no-hitter.

I've never had this problem because I figure as a reporter you must tell people that it is a no-hitter and even—if it's the case—that it's a perfect game. I don't think superstition has anything to do with it, or that anything I say is going to affect what happens on the field.

Anyway, we got to the late innings of this game and, of course, I was talking on the air about the perfect game. And I found out later that Bunning was talking about it in the dugout. He was trying to take the pressure off himself by talking about the fact that he had this perfect game going.

When he got the side out in the eighth, you can imagine how the tension had built up at this point. All

the people in Shea Stadium were well aware of what
was happening. The interesting thing now was that the
Mets fans—and most of them were Mets fans—were
actually pulling for Bunning to pitch the perfect game.

With the score 6–0 in favor of the Phils, he had
enough of a margin he was going to win the ballgame
so the fans would much rather see him win it with a
perfect game. By the ninth inning, they were all on
their feet cheering every pitch. Charlie Smith led off by
fouling out to Bobby Wine, who had come in to play
shortstop at this time.

Now Bunning had just two outs to go for a perfect
game. Everybody was standing up by then. The Mets
sent up a pinch hitter, George Altman, who was a good
left-handed hitter, and the tension was amazing. We
were on TV and we were playing back almost every
pitch on videotape.

Bunning still had this curve ball going and there
seemed no doubt he'd get his perfect game, but still
there was the tension. He struck out Altman for the
26th straight man retired and so far the only tough play
of the game was on Gonder in the fifth.

Just one out to go!

The Mets sent up Johnny Stephenson, who was their
last left-handed hitter, because in a situation like that
you had to continue playing the percentages. Even
though you might in your own heart want a guy to
make it since he has gone this far, you've still got to
give him the greatest obstacles you can.

Bunning ran the count to 2–2 on Stephenson. Then
he threw that third strike past him for his 10th strikeout
and the perfect game and the place was utter bedlam.

Bunning's wife Mary and eldest daughter Barbara,
then 12, had driven up from their home in Cherry Hill,
Pennsylvania, for the game. They both ran on the field

when it was over and were interviewed along with Bunning by the radio, TV and press people.

I didn't talk to Bunning after the game. Ralph Kiner went down for us and interviewed him on the field.

I'd have to say that would have to rank as the game I'll never forget not only because it was a perfect game but because it was a tremendous achievement from other standpoints. After all, here was a guy who had pitched a no-hitter in the American League and now went into the record books as one of the few guys who pitched no-hitters in both leagues.

The only other man to do it was Cy Young, who pitched no-hitters for Cleveland, then in the National League, in 1897, and for Boston in the American League in 1904 and 1905.

Anytime you see a guy making a run at the record book it has to be exciting.

Photo by Clifton Boutelle

AL OLIVER

Outfielder-first baseman Al Oliver didn't labor in total ob-scurity during his 18–year (1968–85) career, but he was usu-ally in the shadow of some more publicized star such as Willie Stargell during his 10 seasons as a Pittsburgh Pirate. Yet Oliver led the National League in batting with .331 in 1983, achieved a .303 career batting average, and shares the American League record for most total bases (21) in a dou-bleheader with the great Jimmie Foxx.

I played in the '71 World Series for the Pittsburgh Pirates but that wasn't too exciting for me because at the time I was being platooned and I was totally against it.

For some reason when I came up to the big leagues in '69 they tried to make me believe I couldn't hit left-handed pitchers. I hit them all through the minors and I knew I could hit them in the majors whether I was a left-handed hitter or not. It really never made a difference to me which side a pitcher was throwing from.

I can look back on my career and be glad that I never believed what they told me because if I had I wouldn't be in the big leagues today. But the thing that has been my strong point, aside from my physical conditioning, is the fact I am so strong mentally nobody can tell me how good I am because even I don't know. I know my abilities and shortcomings, but I don't know my limits.

What I'm saying is that I've always wondered why some ballplayers get so much recognition without being deserving of it while others are deserving but are ignored. I've never understood it.

When I was traded to Texas (December 8, 1977) I was glad to get out of Pittsburgh because I never felt I was appreciated there, either by the fans or the management. I could have stayed on at Pittsburgh and gotten my 3,000th hit and nobody would have known about it except me and my wife.

Going to Texas led to one of my most memorable days, the one I really treasure the most. That was Opening Day of 1978 when we played the New York Yankees at Arlington. I got a standing ovation from the crowd after I got a hit my first time at bat. It gave me a feeling I can't describe. I had a good day all around, making some good plays in the outfield. That gave me a lift.

It never happened to me all the years I was in Pittsburgh and it never would have. All those years it was as if I wasn't even there.

I did have some good days at Pittsburgh, though, and I would have to pick one of them as the game that was most memorable, the one I'll never forget.

We had a good club at Pittsburgh in the early '70s. We won the East Division championship five times, missing only in '73 between 1970 and 1975. But for some reason we were always written off in the play-offs, though we had a club that could bounce back. Still, it's true we won the playoffs only once, in '71 when we beat the San Francisco Giants for the National League pennant.

The Giants were favored to win that playoff, maybe because Candlestick Park was considered tough for us. That put the pressure on us. We had to show the people we were deserving of winning.

The series (best-of-five) opened in San Francisco and the Giants won the first game 6–5. But we won the second game, which people might remember because our first baseman, Bob Robertson, hit three home runs. So we did what we had to do, split the two games in Candlestick Park before the series moved to Pittsburgh.

We won the first game in Pittsburgh to take a 2–1 edge in the series, with Robertson hitting another homer and Richie Hebner hitting one as we beat Juan Marichal 2–1.

That brings us to the game I'll never forget, the fourth game of the '71 playoffs (October 8). It was a wild game. I remember that, the Giants knowing they had to win to stay alive and us being determined to get it over with and not be in the position of having to play a fifth game.

Even in the playoffs I was being platooned in center field with Gene Clines, a right-handed hitter. Danny Murtaugh, our manager, seemed convinced I couldn't hit left-handed pitchers, though it's true he also wanted to get Clines, a good hitter, in the lineup as much as possible.

I was in the lineup for the fourth game because Gaylord Perry, a right-hander, was pitching for the Giants. Steve Blass started for us.

With pitchers like Perry and Blass you would've supposed it would be a tight, well-pitched game. It wasn't. The Giants got a run in the first inning, then four more in the second when Chris Speier hit a home run and Willie McCovey hit one with two men on base.

We stayed right with them. We scored a pair in the first inning and three more in the third when Hebner hit his second homer in two days. That made it 5–5 and it stayed that way until the sixth inning.

The thing that was surprising about it was that Giants manager Charlie Fox stayed with Perry until the sixth, though he was struggling all the way. I guess Fox figured that Perry was *his* "money" pitcher and he might as well live and die with him.

But we finally knocked out Perry in the sixth. He left with a man on, a run in and one out, Fox bringing in Jerry Johnson, a young right-hander. Roberto Clemente was the man on base, and he moved to second on a passed ball.

Willie Stargell was at bat and they walked him to get at me, hoping for the doubleplay. I think that always psyches up any hitter when someone pitches around another man to get at him.

I can understand their thinking. They felt Stargell was more of a long ball threat than I was, which was true. But they overlooked one thing. I'm not often a strikeout victim. I was more capable than Stargell of keeping the ball in play. Still, they went with the percentage and the result was that it worked out for us.

Offhand, I can't remember the count when I hit the ball. I just know I hit it good. I still remember Bobby

Bonds, the Giants right fielder, running to the wall and looking helplessly as the ball cleared it for a three-run homer.

Well, I take back what I said earlier. They did cheer me in Pittsburgh once. That was when I hit that homer which won the '71 pennant for us. They cheered and they threw confetti and they appreciated that I'd helped the club.

There are a lot of days at Pittsburgh I'd like to forget, but that one I never will.

CLAUDE PASSEAU

No team has gone as long without appearing in a World Series as the Chicago Cubs, who last played in one in 1945. They lost to the Detroit Tigers, but nobody could fault Claude Passeau, the veteran ace of their pitching staff. Passeau was 17–9 in 1945, and had a record of 162–150 during his 13–season (1935–47) career. He was a 20–game winner in 1940.

I was sheriff of George County here in Mississippi for eight years until 1976 and I enjoyed the job, not that it was easy. But you've always got to be doing something and I guess I've kept busy enough since I retired from baseball more than 30 years ago.

I started a farm equipment business back in 1940 when I was with the Chicago Cubs. It's been a while since I gave it to my boy to run. It's right here in Lucedale (Mississippi) and I still take a hand in it. I like to go in the store, talk to the customers, people I've known a long time. I even pick up and deliver to have something to do.

I had a farm for many years until I sold it in 1960. It was a good-sized place, 640 acres. Had half of it in tung nuts, rest in other crops. Some people don't know what tung nuts are, I suppose, but they used to be a big source of revenue around here. The oil was used as a base for paint and varnish.

So I've kept pretty busy since I've been out of baseball, though I've cut down on work lately. Plenty of time and places to go fishing around this area and I can't think of a better way to enjoy yourself.

I can't say I miss baseball even if I was in it so many years. Don't see many people I used to know in the game. There aren't many around here. Coaches and scouts come through once in a while and we'll have a cup of coffee and shoot the bull. Dizzy Dean was a great friend of mine. He lived about 35 miles from here in Bond, Mississippi. There's a man I miss. It was an honor to be his friend.

Being out of the game 30 years, the people I know in it are few and far between. I've gone to a couple of old timers' games, one in San Diego, another in Chicago. It was nice to see some of the men I played with on the Cubs, like Billy Herman, Phil Cavarretta, Stan Hack and some others.

I've been invited to some other get-togethers like those. People are very nice. They'll say, "Claude, I think we'd really enjoy having you." And I appreciate the honor of being asked. But going causes too durn much confusion and I don't like to travel far. Never did, not even when I was playing ball.

When I got through with playing baseball I sort of closed the door on it. I didn't care too much for it when I was a player. Even when I was in high school I didn't participate in the game. I'd rather fish and hunt. It was strictly a business for me, kind of the way it is for a lot of guys. I'd cut a guy's throat to win, but after it was over I forgot about the game.

About the only time I think about baseball now is during the World Series, or when someone mentions a record that's being broken. There are fans here, but not as rabid as up north. There's just not as much baseball talk, though we get the big league games here on TV Monday nights. I'll sit down and watch one once in a while, but mostly when the sun goes down I'm off fishing. It's not so hot then.

I'll admit there was a time I thought about staying in the game. After I got through playing I thought about umpiring. I wrote to George Barr, the umpire, but it didn't come to anything so I decided to stay down here and tend to my business and I've never been sorry.

Like I said, there's not much baseball talk here except around World Series time. Then once in a while we'll get to talking about the '45 Series when I pitched for the Cubs. That does bring a lot of things to mind. I pitched in three games of that Series against the Detroit Tigers.

I wouldn't say the '45 Cubs were a great team, but they were a good team. They were good enough to win the National League pennant and when you can do that you don't have to apologize. Some of our players had great years, like Cavarretta and Hank Borowy. I had one of my better years (17–9). We went into the Series knowing we could win.

Of course, I went into every game to win. It never occurred to me that I wouldn't win. I never thought about losing, but I lost some good ones. I remember one game I lost. It was the 1941 All-Star Game. I was pitching for the National League when Ted Williams hit a home run in the ninth with two men on and two out to beat us 7–5.

But it's two games in that '45 World Series I remember best. One of them we won, the other we lost. I like to think that maybe if I hadn't got hurt in that second game I pitched we might have beat the Tigers in the Series.

I started the third game against the Tigers (October 5, 1945, at Detroit), with the Series even at a game apiece. I don't know if I ever had better stuff than I had in that game. All my pitches were working: forkball, curve ball, knuckleball, fastball. I never had better control.

Rudy York poked a single to left off me in the second inning and that's the only hit the Tigers got as we beat them 3–0. I walked a man in the sixth, so there were only two men on base in the whole game. That was only the second one-hitter that had been pitched in a Series up to that time and, of course, it was long before Don Larsen's perfect game for the Yankees.

People who remind me of that one-hitter don't realize that I pitched just about as well a few days later in the sixth game until I was injured. If there's a game I'd have to pick out as the one I'll never forget it would have to be that one.

We were leading 5–1 in the seventh and I had a two-hitter when Jimmy Outlaw stepped up to hit. I threw him a knuckleball on which he broke his bat. The ball came through the box and I stuck my pitching hand in front of it. I knocked the ball down, but it ripped the nail of my middle finger.

I tried to continue pitching, but I couldn't grip the ball right. The Tigers got a couple of more hits off me, and I walked some men. I had to leave the game.

Even when I left we were leading 5–3, but our relief pitching couldn't hold the Tigers and the game was tied after eight innings 7–7. We had to win the game to keep the Series alive because Detroit was leading three games to two so Manager Charlie Grimm brought in Borowy, who had started the previous day and lost.

Borowy came through, holding the Tigers hitless the next four innings. In the 12th, we scored the winning run. With two out and a runner on first, Hack hit a single to left. The ball struck a sprinkling system faucet and bounced over left fielder Hank Greenberg's head. While Greenberg was chasing the ball, the runner from first scored and we won the game 8–7 in 12 innings.

Grimm felt he was forced to start Borowy the next day in the seventh game. But he didn't have a thing, having pitched in the previous two games and before the first inning was over Detroit led 5–0. They won the game and the Series.

A lot of people thought if I hadn't been hurt in the sixth game Borowy would have had an extra day's rest and we could have won the Series.

It was a hit off the bat of Outlaw that I remember most of all because it may have cost us the World Series.

Outlaw lives in Jackson, Alabama, about 65 to 70 miles from here. Haven't seen him in many years, but I guess we'd talk about that if we ever got together.

Photo by Ron Mrowiec

TONY PEREZ

An All-Star selection both as a first baseman and third base-
man, Tony Perez contributed heavily to the Cincinnati Reds'
success in the 1970s. Perez drove in 100 or more runs seven
times during his 23–year (1964–86) career, and for 12 con-
secutive seasons drove in 90 or more runs. His peak year
might have been 1970 when he hit .317 with 40 home runs
and 129 runs batted in. He managed the Reds briefly in 1993.

For me, it is not difficult to think of one game that was my greatest thrill. When somebody asks, right away I remember the All-Star Game of 1967 at Anaheim (California) where so many batters struck out.

I did not expect to play in the All-Star Game that year. I never thought I'd make it. That season the Reds moved me to play third base after I had played first base my first two years at Cincinnati.

It was not a strange position for me, third base, because that is where I played in the minor leagues. But when I went to third base again in 1967 it made me think I would not be on the All-Star team. There were third basemen like Richie Allen at Philadelphia and Ron Santo at Chicago who would be ahead of me.

Like I thought, when the National League All-Star team was announced Richie Allen was voted the third baseman. That did not surprise me. And I thought Walter Alston would choose Santo as the other third baseman. But he did not. He named me. That surprised me.

Let me say, it thrilled me, too. Some people act like it makes no difference being chosen to the All-Star team. I didn't feel like that. It was a great honor to me, a great thrill. My third year in the major leagues and chosen to the All-Star team. I was just happy to go, even if I didn't play.

My wife, Petuka, was just as excited as me. We went to Anaheim together with our son, Victor Manuel, who was just a year old then. We were delayed and we didn't get to the hotel until late the night before the game.

When I went up to the registration desk in the Grand Hotel the clerk looked through the reservations and said, "Perez? Perez? We have no reservation under that name. I'm sorry, I don't have a room for you, Mr. Perez. We're filled up."

I could not believe it. "But I am here to play in the All-Star Game tomorrow. There must be some mistake. You must have a room."

The clerk looked at me and said, "Well, Mr. Perez, if you would wait a moment maybe we can solve your problem."

He talked to someone and came back. "We can give you the President's Suite, if that's all right. We were holding it for Mr. Alston, and he said he won't be needing it because he lives in the Los Angeles area."

Naturally I said, "That's okay, we'll take it," and with my family I hurried up to the President's Suite. Can you imagine me, Tony Perez, in the President's Suite? My wife and I were so excited we could hardly sleep. There we were living like the President."

The next day, July 11, 1967, was the All-Star Game. It did not start until 4:15 in the afternoon because it would be better for television on the East Coast. There was a lot of talk about how it would make it tough on the hitters to start at that time. The pitchers would be throwing out of the shadows by the fourth and fifth innings.

I was on the bench when the game started and never really expected I would play. Allen was at third base and the way the game went I didn't think Alston, who was managing the National League team, would make a change.

Right from the beginning you could see it would be a tough day for the batters even though they turned the lights on to cut down the shadows. When Allen hit a home run off Dean Chance of the American League in the second inning it looked like that might be the only run of the game.

Juan Marichal, who started for the National League, struck out three men in the three innings he pitched and Ferguson Jenkins, who pitched the next three innings, struck out six. But Brooks Robinson hit a home run off Jenkins in the sixth to tie the game 1–1.

That was all the runs for nine innings. If the game had ended in regulation time I would never have gotten to play. Not that I would have been unhappy. I was just glad to be sitting there on the bench at an All-Star Game.

The strikeouts kept piling up. At first it was because it was hazy and the shadows made the ball hard to see. Later it was because everybody was taking the big swing. Roberto Clemente struck out four times. Can you imagine that?

When the game was over the National League players had struck out 17 times, the American League players 13.

I struck out, too. It happened after Alston surprised me by sending me in to play for Allen in the 10th inning. Catfish Hunter was pitching for the American League. He set me up with breaking balls my first time up then struck me out on a fastball. I remembered that the next time I came to bat.

When the 15th inning started it looked for a moment like Orlando Cepeda was going to get the big hit for us. He drove a pitch by Hunter deep and high to right field but Tony Conigliaro got back to the wall and pulled it down.

Funny thing, Conigliaro also had robbed Cepeda of a big hit in the 10th inning. If he hadn't made those two catches on Cepeda I wouldn't have gotten my chance to do a big thing.

But Conigliaro made the big play on Cepeda again in the 15th and I came up to face Hunter. I was thinking, "Just wait for your pitch and hit it. Don't be over-anxious."

The first pitch was a breaking ball on the corner and I took it. I figured he'd come on the outside again with a fastball. It felt good as soon as I hit it. I knew it was out, high and deep to left field.

Not that I saw it go. I was just running the bases, but the people were telling me by the way they cheered.

I felt like a President. I'd slept in the President's Suite and now I'd hit the home run to put the National League ahead 2–1.

Tom Seaver got the American League out in the bottom half of the 15th and we won the game.

Afterwards the reporters came to ask me how I felt and I couldn't tell them, I felt so good. I lived like the President one night and that was something, wasn't it?

Photo courtesy of New York Yankees

LOU PINIELLA

In 18 seasons (1964, 1968–84) as a player, Lou Piniella earned a reputation as a dependable outfielder, mostly with the Kansas City Royals and New York Yankees. He played in four World Series as a Yankee. and finished with a .291 career batting average. Piniella later was a successful manager of the Cincinnati Reds, the Yankees and the Seattle Mariners. His Reds won the World Series in 1990.

When you've been around playing as long as I have, things sort of fall into perspective and you come to realize what this game of baseball is all about.

That's winning, of course. And the more you see of the game, the longer you play, the better you understand what it takes to make a team a winner. I suppose it is only natural that so much is made of individual feats, personal records and achievements, but I've found that over the long haul they only matter so far as they contribute to the team record.

It has been my experience that when everybody is playing together, when everybody is picking the other guy up, that's when you win, no matter even if the individual statistic may not be as spectacular as those of some players on teams that are not doing as well.

When you get older and look back on your career and reminisce, if you look at things from the standpoint I've been talking about, you tend to think of the big games as being the ones that the team won, not games that were big individually. That's what baseball is all about. Even though you use individual effort to get the job done, the team aspect, the blend of individuals working toward a common goal, makes for success in the game.

Oh sure, I've had some days here and there in 14 years in the big leagues that I felt were outstanding individually. The home runs, the winning RBI, the plays you make in the field and the throws, all those make an impact at the time and give you a feeling of achievement.

And getting an award such as the Rookie of the Year in 1969 when I came up with the Kansas City Royals is a great honor. You get a great deal of satisfaction from something like that.

I've been fortunate in my career. In 14 full years in the big leagues (including 1982), I've been on two World Series winners, four American League pennant winners, five American League East division winners, all with the New York Yankees.

That means I've played in a lot of big games, a lot of games that stand out during the stretch run of a season, during the league playoffs and in the World Series. Some of them are truly outstanding, like the one in which Chris Chambliss hit the home run against Kansas City in 1976 to win the American League pennant, and the one in the World Series in which Reggie Jackson hit three home runs against the Los Angeles Dodgers in 1977.

But one game stands out above all the others for me. And if you talk to any of the players on our ball club that have been with the Yankees for a number of years and ask them which game stands out the most you invariably come down to one game—against the Boston Red Sox in 1978.

That was one season that stands out in particular for me because it shows what can happen when a team plays together. We were 14 games behind Boston in mid-July and a lot of people thought we were out of it. But then we started to play and we moved up on them. Everything fell into place and everybody picked up everybody.

We caught the Red Sox on the final day of the season and tied them for first. Both clubs had 99 wins and so we were forced into a one-game playoff for the right to continue on to play the West Division winners, Kansas City, for the American League pennant, and hopefully on to the World Series.

It was a beautiful, fresh, cool afternoon at Fenway Park (October 4, 1978), and I still remember the excitement that seemed to surround everyone—the players, the crowd. Everything on the line in one game—you can't ask for anything more than that if you want a dramatic finish.

I was in right field that day and I remember thinking, "Well, it's all come down to this. Who could have believed it in July when we were 14 games back?"

Both clubs had the starting pitchers they wanted in there, Ron Guidry for us, Mike Torrez for Boston. I can't believe any pitcher ever had a better season than Guidry had that year. He was 24–3 going into that play-off game. Torrez, a big, strong right-hander, had won 15 games.

We had a chance to score in the first but didn't. I remember bouncing out on a grounder with a man on second.

The Red Sox jumped off to an early lead. Carl Yastrzemski hit a home run in the second inning. I got a single to lead off the fourth—it was a slow bouncer in the infield that I beat out—but Torrez got the next three men. He was really pitching well. You could see he was up for the game. I hit a fly deep to center off him in the sixth, but it wasn't a tough chance for Fred Lynn, who was playing center.

Boston scored another run in the sixth to make it 2–0 and the way Torrez was pitching those two runs looked like they might be enough.

There were a couple of singles—I think by Chambliss and Roy White—but there were two out when Bucky Dent came to bat in the seventh. I remember hoping he would poke one through the infield for a single so we could get at least a run, anything to break through to keep the inning going.

On Torrez's second pitch, Dent fouled the ball off his left foot and hobbled around a while. He even went back to the dugout to get a new bat—I think he borrowed one from Roy White.

The next pitch—that's the one he hit into that left field screen for a three-run homer to put us ahead 3–2. I can't think of a home run I've seen as exciting as that one and I've seen a lot of them hit farther and harder. But that was the big one.

We scored another run that inning to make it 4–2 and Jackson hit a homer in the eighth to make it 5–2.

The Red Sox finally got to Guidry in the seventh but Goose Gossage, who had been doing it all season, worked out of that jam. They did get a pair of runs off Gossage in the eighth and then had the tying and winning runs on in the ninth with Yastrzemski up.

You sort of hold your breath in a situation like that and with a batter as good as Yastrzemski up there. But Gossage handled him. Yaz popped to third and that was it. We had won the American League East title and were going to play Kansas City for the pennant.

Anytime anybody ask me about the game I'll never forget, the most exciting game I've ever played in, etc. . . etc. . . that's the only one in my mind.

I didn't get a big hit and I don't remember any spectacular play in the field that I made though I played quite well and made some nice plays in the outfield.

But because of what it meant to the team, because of what was at stake, that game, in my mind, by far exceeds any other game I could possibly even think about.

Photo courtesy of *Baseball Digest*

DAN QUISENBERRY

Famed for his whimsical wit almost as much as his pitching skill, Dan Quisenberry was an outstanding closer during his 12-season (1979–1990) career, most of it spent with the Kansas City Royals. Quisenberry led the American League in saves five times, with a career-high of 45 in 1983 after recording 44 the previous season.

I don't really like to brag on myself. I like to brag on other guys. That's just the way I feel about it.

Sure, there are all kinds of games that I've pitched that are memorable to me, sometimes for what I've done, but mostly for what they meant to our team, or for what other players did in them.

I've been in all sorts of pennant races when I was with the Kansas City Royals. I've pitched in two World Series, three American League championship playoffs, and even in a division title playoff, in 1981 when we lost to the Oakland A's for the American League West championship.

Any number of those games could stand out for me, and there are many other ones, such as my 45th save in 1983 to set the record (American League, since surpassed) for most saves.

There's not a lot of thrills that could top or even match being on a World Series winner, which happened to me with the Royals in 1985. Or disappointments, like the one in '80 when we lost the World Series to the Philadelphia Phillies.

And for a pitcher to be the winner in a World Series game is something you always dream of. When you do it, it's a dream come true and I was the winning pitcher in a game in each of the '80 and '85 World Series.

The sixth game of the '85 Series against the St. Louis Cardinals (October 26, 1985, at Kansas City) is one game that neither I or most people, players or fans, will ever forget. That was the one with the controversy over umpire Don Denkinger's decision at first base on the Cardinals in the ninth inning.

St. Louis was leading 1–0 with the bases loaded and two out in the eighth inning when I came in to relieve Charlie Leibrandt. The batter was Willie McGee and he hit a grounder to Frank White, who got the force at second to end the threat.

We didn't score in the bottom of the eighth and St. Louis didn't score in the ninth so it was still 1–0 in its favor going into the bottom of the inning.

Our leadoff man, pinch hitter Jorge Orta, hit a chopper to the right side that was fielded by first baseman Jack Clark. He tossed the ball to the pitcher, Todd Worrell, covering first. It was a bang-bang play and Denkinger ruled Orta safe. That set off a helluva argument by the Cardinals, but it didn't do them any good and Orta's single had opened the door for us.

Before it was over, Dane Iorg got a pinch-hit single with one out in the ninth to drive in two runs and we'd won 2–1. I was the winning pitcher, and that was a thrill, but nothing compared to the next day when we went on to win the seventh game 11–0 and earn a World Series ring.

Until you've been on a World Series winner you can't imagine the feeling of accomplishment and of unity.

It's the greatest feeling in the world, the ultimate in baseball. And no individual accomplishment can match it. It's a team game and as a team player you get the most satisfaction out of team accomplishments. I know that I do.

Like I said, I don't like to brag about myself. I like to be a normal guy trying to do his best. I don't even like to be praised. I don't feel as good about that as hearing my teammates praised. I like to brag about other guys.

And of all the games I've been in the most memorable is the one in which the "other guy" did something great. He gave me, he gave all of us on the Royals, the greatest moment I've ever experienced in baseball.

That came in the third game of the 1980 American League Championship Series against the New York Yankees. We'd won the first two games in our own park and now the third game (October 10) was in Yankee Stadium.

I guess we had a score to settle with the Yankees. They'd beaten the Royals in three previous playoffs (1976, '77 and '78) and you always had the feeling though we were leading two games-to-nothing (best-of-five series) they could come back.

In Game 3 we scored a run off Tommy John in the fifth on a home run by White, but when I relieved Paul Splittorff in the bottom of the sixth there was one out and Reggie Jackson was on second base with a double.

Oscar Gamble hit a grounder to the right of (second baseman) White, who saw he had no play at first so he threw to third. But he threw it over George's (Brett) head for an error and Jackson scored to tie the game 1–1. It was the right play, but the throw was errant and Gamble went all the way to thrid.

Rick Cerone then drove in Gamble with a single and the Yankees led 2–1.

The crowd noise was just deafening. The way the crowd was going you'd have thought the Yankees already had won the game. It was just overwhelming.

In our half of the seventh, Willie Wilson doubled with two out. The Yankees brought in Goose Gossage. He'd blown the Royals away all year. He was the hardest thrower I've ever seen. And the crowd was going wild the moment he got to the mound.

But U.L. Washington beat out an infield hit and that brought up Brett. This was strength against strength. And Brett won. He hit the first pitch by Goose, a bomb to right field, a three-run homer that put us ahead 4–2.

The fans had been going crazy. But all of a sudden you couldn't hear a sound.

That moment was the greatest moment I've ever experienced in baseball. It was just electric. We won that game 4–2 to go into the World Series.

That's the game I'll never forget. I've never experienced anything like the instant George hit that home run.

PEE WEE REESE

At the heart of the team remembered fondly as "The Boys of Summer" was shortstop Pee Wee Reese, a model of consistency and durability. No other tribute is required other than to note that Reese played in seven World Series for the Brooklyn Dodger despite losing three seasons to military service during World War II. Reese's career extended from 1940 to 1958. He was inducted into the Hall of Fame in 1984.

I know there are a number of games I'll never forget but there's one I sure would rather forget. I try to get it out of my mind but can't which sure singles it out as the game I'll never forget even if I want to.

I guess by now most of you know the game I'm talking about. I've seen a lot of accounts of that game and I guess about a million people were in the old Polo Grounds in New York when Bobby Thomson hit the home run for the New York Giants that beat us, the Brooklyn Dodgers. And I guess about 500 million people heard it on the air—or at least I think so from all the people who claim to have.

I'd rather talk about another game, the one in which we won the 1955 World Series over the New York Yankees. I played against the Yankees in five previous Series with the Brooklyn Dodgers and they always beat us up in them. Here I was, 35, 36 years old, and it looked like I'd never be on a World Series winner.

So when we beat the Yankees in the '55 Series it probably was my biggest thrill in baseball. It had to be.

Sure, that's the game I'd rather talk about but I'd be kidding somebody if I was to pick it as the game I'll never forget. Only one game really stands out from all the rest and you can't get away from it—much as I'd like to. That's the third game of the National League playoffs in 1951, on October 3 between the Giants and Dodgers.

I've seen a lot of things about how the Dodgers "blew" the pennant that year because we had a 13½-game lead over the Giants in August. Now I know that's not fair. Sure, we were way out ahead and it looked like the way we were playing we'd win by 20 or 25 games.

What made it really seem like a sure thing is that we had gotten in front although we had a little problem in left field for a while. Then we got Andy Pafko from the Cubs to play there and he was quite a player.

At the time nobody could understand how the Cubs could let us have a player like Pafko. With him, we had a club a lot like the Cincinnati Reds in 1970—solid all around. If we were behind in the eighth or ninth innings our fellows just thought we were going to win anyway.

It looked sure but it didn't work out that way. We played well enough, winning 26 of our last 48 games. But the Giants won 37 of their last 44 and we finished up the regular season tied for first. So nobody can say we collapsed. We were playing pretty well—it's just that the Giants played incredibly for such a long stretch as 44 games.

So we went into the best-of-three games playoffs, starting at Ebbets Field. The Giants won the first game 3–1. A lot of people have forgotten an interesting point about that opening game—that Bobby Thomson hit a two-run homer off Ralph Branca! It's funny, but nobody remembers that home run.

We bounced right back the next day with Clem Labine pitching and beat the Giants 10–0 so the playoffs was even at a victory apiece. It all had come down to that final game on October 3 at the Polo Grounds.

We were still confident. We had Don Newcombe pitching for us and he'd won 20 games for us in the regular season. The Giants started Sal Maglie, who had won 23. We had a little luck going for us and Thomson, who was playing third, had a difficult day in the field so we got a run in the first and three more in the eighth to take a 4–1 lead.

Newcombe, if I remember correctly, struck out the side in the eighth. But when he came into the dugout he told Charlie Dressen, the manager, "It looks like I don't have it anymore. Better get me out of there, Skipper."

But Jackie Robinson and one of the other players talked Newk into going back and pitching the ninth inning. So he went back out and it seemed like nothing was right after that. Things began to happen.

I know Alvin Dark led off with a hard grounder to the right side and Gil Hodges left first base to go after it. Robinson, at second, came up with the ball but there was nobody at first to throw to. The next hit, by Don Mueller, was almost the same and the Giants had two men on.

I don't remember being worried and I guess it eased up a little when Monte Irvin, the Giants' big man, fouled out. But then came Whitey Lockman and he drove a double to left field and that scored a run and now the Giants had the tying runs on base with just one out and the score 4–2.

Dressen called the bullpen and asked who was ready. They had Labine down there, but he had pitched the day before. Preacher Roe was throwing, too. But they said that the man that was really ready to come in was Branca, who had lost the first game to the Giants. So Branca came in to pitch to Thomson.

Branca threw the first pitch, a fastball, over the inside corner where Rube Walker, who was catching, wanted it. It was a called strike. Then Walker tried to get Branca to throw another fastball up and in on Thomson to push him back a little bit. But he didn't get it in far enough, got it over the plate, and Thomson hit it into the stands in left.

I can still remember standing at shortstop thinking to myself, "We must have another chance to win this game." I looked at the scoreboard and it dawned on me this was it, that we had lost, that there were no chances left.

I saw Bobby Thomson circle the bases and—for some reason or other—sort of in a dream caught Eddie Stanky running down to third base and tackling Leo (Durocher), jumping all over Leo, and Leo trying to get away to get to Thomson.

I swear I don't really remember how I got to the clubhouse or anything about it. But I know when I first got to the clubhouse I saw Ralph Branca sitting on the steps crying like a baby. You couldn't blame him. A lot of us felt the same way about it to tell the truth.

From time to time, people remind me about that game, but they don't bother me too much. I know it didn't stay with me. But it did hurt Branca. I don't think he ever was the same after that and it is sad. He was a young fellow with great potential—already had won 20 games—and this hurt him. I understand that he still has to live with it, that people even bring it up to his children.

Even though I try to forget that game there's no chance for me to do it. I've heard Russ Hodges' voice so often on replays of the moment Thomson hit the home run. "We win it, we win it, we win it," he keeps saying over and over again.

So if there's any game I'd rather forget that would be the one—but you know I never will.

Photo by Ron Mrowiec

RICK REUSCHEL

*A big, soft-spoken farm boy, Rick Reuschel had virtually two
careers as a major leaguer from 1972 to 1991. He was a winning pitcher on mostly losing Chicago Cubs teams for the
first 10 seasons, reaching a high of 20–10 in 1977. After re-
covering from arm problems, he enjoyed several more good
years with the Pittsburgh Pirates and San Francisco Giants,
helping the latter win a National League pennant in 1989.*

There's only one game that stands out for me, though it's not the one most people think about when I'm asked about the highlights of my career.

Maybe one of these days the Cubs will get into the playoffs and the World Series and I'll have a game to remember that really means something from a team standpoint. I sure hope so because our fans have been waiting a long time and they've given us great support. I hope we can win it for them.

One game most people refer to in conversation with me is the one in '75 in which my brother Paul and I combined to pitch a shutout over the Los Angeles Dodgers. Maybe it doesn't mean as much as it should because Paul didn't get credit for a save. That sort of took some of the satisfaction out of it.

What made the game so unusual was that it was the first time in baseball history two brothers had combined in pitching a shutout. After the game, the writers checked and said there was no record of a similar performance.

At the time I was having some problems with chronic blisters on the index finger of my pitching hand. Every six weeks or so a blister would show up and I'd need relief even when I was pitching well.

In this game we had a 3–0 lead in the seventh inning when the blister started bothering me. It wasn't real bad, but if I'd kept pitching it would have broken open. Manager Jim Marshall didn't want to take a chance on losing me for two weeks so he brought in Paul with one out in the seventh.

Paul had just come up from the Wichita farm club a few weeks before and had pitched real well in relief. It made me happy to have my brother on the team and doing so well.

In this game he couldn't have been better. He pitched two and two-thirds innings, giving up just one hit and we won 6–0. I got the win, but Paul didn't get a save because he was one hitter short of pitching three full innings after coming in with a five-run lead.

I might have remembered the game better if Paul had gotten the save. I suppose it should have been enough that it was unique, the only time brothers had combined for a shutout. But Paul not getting something to show for it on his record book took a little out of it for me.

The other game I mentioned, the one I'll never forget isn't a game I won. I lost and it was my own fault, but it was one of the best games I've ever pitched. I don't think I've ever been "in a game" as much as I was that night at Houston (June 4, 1976).

The Cubs have never had much luck in the Astrodome. I've never quite figured out why. It seems to me it's darker in there than in other places, though I'm not sure it is. It may be just imagination on my part. But whatever the reason, the Astros really have hurt us there ever since I've been a Cub. We've always had trouble getting used to playing in there.

I had good stuff that night, and pitched real good. But so did Mike Cosgrove for the Astros. We worked fast, which really keeps you "in" a game. It helps your concentration. You don't have time to let your mind wander. It keeps everybody on their toes, makes for a batter game all around, including the fielders, who'll come up with more outstanding plays.

We had a chance to break out in front in the first inning when Rick Monday led off with a double, but Cosgrove bore down and got the side out.

Cesar Cedeno laid down a bunt in the Astros' first, and it was perfect, rolling dead on the artificial turf, which is something unusual. Neither Bill Madlock, the third baseman, or I had a chance on it. I didn't think anything of it and got out of the inning without trouble.

In the Astros' second, Jose Cruz topped a ball and it rolled in front of the plate. I had the best shot at it so I picked it up and tried to get him at first base. My throw was wild and got past our first baseman, Larry Biittner, to roll down the right field line. Cruz went to third.

I didn't think I was off balance when I threw to first, but I guess I was. I probably shouldn't have thrown it but anytime you get a ball hit like that you don't know where the runner is.

When I picked up the ball I looked up and I thought, "Holy Cow, there he is already, almost at first." But I threw anyway. Sometimes when you do make the throw and it's a good one the ump gives you the call.

Anyway, Cruz went to third and scored when Enos Cabell bounced out. That was the only run of the game.

One run that early doesn't mean much and I was pitching good. In fact, I didn't give up another hit. I think I walked a couple of men in the seventh and that's all the Astros could get off me.

There might have been more hits but I had great fielding behind me. Jose Cardenal made a great catch of a liner by Greg Gross to left and Manny Trillo went behind second base to throw out Rob Andrews on what looked like a sure hit.

But we couldn't get lucky against Cosgrove. We even loaded the bases in the fifth inning without scoring a run. Like most of the time in the Astrodome, we just couldn't keep anything going.

The ninth inning was just like the rest for us. Jerry Morales led off with a single, but then the next batter hit into a doubleplay, and Cosgrove got the last out on a pop-up.

The strange thing about it was that though the game was over, the Astros winning 1–0, I didn't realize it right away.

The game was going so fast and I was so into it that I ran out to the mound to pitch what I thought would be the bottom of the ninth. Not until I saw that I was the only guy on the field did I realize the game was over and we'd lost.

JERRY REUSS

Left-hander Jerry Reuss enjoyed a respectable and extended career of 22 seasons (1969–1990) in which he posted a 220–191 record mainly as a starter for the Pittsburgh Pirates and Los Angeles Dodgers. Reuss three times won 18 games in a season, and his best campaign came in 1980 when he was 18–6 for the Dodgers and led the National League in shutouts with six.

Actually, there are three games that stand out and I
don't know that I can separate them on what they
mean to me. They're the no-hitter, the playoff game
against the Houston Astros in '81 and the fifth game of
the World Series against the New York Yankees in '81.

From a personal standpoint, I guess I'd have to
choose the no-hitter I pitched for the Los Angeles
Dodgers against the San Francisco Giants at Candlestick Park (June 27, 1980).

One thing that stands out for me is that it was hot—
not warm but really hot—something you don't often
see in San Francisco in June. Usually the fans are sitting
there bundled up, but they were in T-shirts and shorts
that night.

I don't remember that I felt anything special warm-
ing-up before the game. They say sometimes you can
tell when you've got "no-hitter stuff." In this case, I
don't recall anything special about my pitches other
than I kept them low and spotted the ball real well,
worked the corners.

In the first inning, one man got on on an error, but
that was it. That's how close I came to a perfect game.
There were no spectacular plays, everything was rou-
tine. I struck out two men, and the hardest hit ball was
a foul—by Terry Whitfield, a pinch hitter. It was about
a foot foul past third base and that's about as close as
anybody came to a hit.

That no-hitter was a big lift for me and my career at
the time because the year before I'd been struggling
(7–14 in 1979) and had started the '80 season in the
bullpen. I had pitched pretty well in relief and got back
to starting in mid-May, done well, and the no-hitter
sort of confirmed my confidence in a new pitching
style.

Early in my career I was a high-ball pitcher, but at
this point (1980) I began to keep everything down. I

had much better extension than I had earlier in my career and I felt much stronger. It was like a turning point in my career.

The other two games I'll never forget came in the '81 "player's strike" season when they had a split-season format in which the winner of each half of the season met in a best-of-five games playoff for the division title before the division winners played for the league pennants.

We really got ourselves in the hole against the Astros by losing the first two games. I started the second game and pitched a shutout for nine innings but we lost it 1–0 in 11.

You can imagine the tension at that point. It really had built up. Another loss and we were out. But we got some good pitching and timely hitting and we evened the series at 2–2.

I started the fifth game (October 11, at Los Angeles), and my opponent was Nolan Ryan, who had beaten us with a two-hitter in the opener and pitched a no-hitter against us a few weeks earlier.

I felt the pressure like anybody else would. A do-or-die situation and you just hope you can hold them until your teammates can get some timely hits.

That's just what happened. We held them and finally broke through against Ryan for three runs in the sixth inning and went on to win 4–0. I had a five-hitter, but what I remember most was the final out of the game.

I had two strikes on the final batter, Dave Roberts, and I did something I never had done before. I began to rub up the ball, got off to the back of the mound and just turned around and looked at all those 55,000 frenzied fans.

This was the kind of situation you dream about when you're six or eight years old, going for the final out in a game that means a title. Here it was for me!

I finally got back on the mound and threw a pitch that hit the dirt at which Roberts swung for the third strike. It went all the way back to the screen with the catcher, Mike Scioscia, chasing it.

Roberts finally realized he could go for first base, but Scioscia threw all the way from the screen and I can still see all five feet eight inches of Steve Garvey (first baseman) stretching as far as he could to take the throw for the final out of that series.

We'd fought from behind, like we had all season, and it was just a great moment.

The National League Championship Series against the Montreal Expos was another struggle, and we won it in five games, which put us in the World Series against the Yankees.

Just as we had all season, we got in the hole again by losing the first two games to the Yankees. I pitched the opener but it wasn't one of my better starts, and we lost the second game, too.

But then we won two straight to even the World Series at 2–2, and Manager Tommy Lasorda handed me the ball for the fifth game (October 25, 1981, at Los Angeles), with a chance to put us ahead.

I can't say I had my best stuff that day. I wiggled out of one jam after another. But the Yankees got just one run off me, in the second inning. It was a battle, and if you remember, that's the game in which Ron Cey got hit in the head by a pitch, which gave everybody a scare. Luckily, he was all right.

We finally broke through when Pedro Guerrero and Steve Yeager hit back-to-back home runs in the seventh inning. That 2–1 lead stood up.

With two out in the ninth, a man on base and Aurelio Rodriguez at bat with two strikes on him, I did just what I had done against Houston. I rubbed the ball and looked around at the crowd. Then I stepped back onto the mound and struck him out.

We went on to win the World Series after being down two games to none just as we had come back against the Astros.

Those three games, they're the ones that stand out for me.

Photo by Frank Bryan

BROOKS ROBINSON

No third baseman surpassed Brooks Robinson in fielding ability during his 23–year (1955–77) career, all with the Baltimore Orioles. Robinson set many major league fielding marks, but also swung a potent bat, with 268 career home runs. He won the American League Most Valuable Player Award in 1964 when he batted .317 with 28 home runs and 118 runs batted in.

I'll never forget the exciting days right before my graduation from Little Rock (Arkansas) Senior High School in May 1955. Twelve of the then 16 major league clubs were interested in varying degrees in signing me and it was a lot of fun trying to decide which offer to take.

I'd just turned 18 a few days before graduation and since I had been a little kid all summer long I had either practiced or played baseball. We didn't have a high school team but an American Legion team filled the gap.

I played basketball on our high school team and one year we went all the way to the semifinals in the state tournament. We lost by just one point to undefeated Jonesboro. I played basketball well enough to be offered a scholarship by the University of Arkansas.

So when the major league scouts came around I was torn between going to college or trying to make it in baseball. Luckily, as it turned out, I chose baseball and have been fortunate enough to be successful in the game.

But May 29, 1955, the day after graduation, was an exciting one. My Dad and I weighed several offers, including one from Baltimore which included a $4,000 bonus. We slept on the offer, but the next morning I made my decision, signing with Baltimore and have never regretted it.

The Orioles at the time were a young team in a building program and I figured I had a good chance to make the major leagues in three years, the period I had set as my goal.

Immediately after signing, I went to Baltimore and spent two weeks with the Orioles just getting acquainted. I didn't get to play but I did work out with the club and got to go on a road trip. The Orioles then sent me to York (Pennsylvania), their class B farm team in the Piedmont League.

I got off to a good start in professional baseball. I hit .331 at York and felt I was making real progress. I felt even better about it when after the Piedmont League season ended the Orioles called me up to finish out the season with them.

Naturally, I didn't figure I'd get much of a chance to play with the Orioles. Paul Richards, who then was managing Baltimore, had told me before sending me to York that he "liked what I saw" but that he'd like me to get experience.

But I'll have to admit I was pretty excited when I got to Baltimore on Saturday (September 16, 1955). I went right to the ballpark because the Orioles were playing a game with Washington. I got into uniform and chose a good spot in the dugout to watch the game. I didn't figure on being anything other than a spectator.

I was just sitting there, minding my own business, when coach Lum Harris came over to me. I wasn't even thinking about getting in the lineup because Don Leppert was the regular third baseman. But Harris surprised me.

"Leppert's not feeling well," Harris said. "Get your glove, Robbie, you're on third."

I was a little shaky as I went out to the infield to warm up. Looking back, I guess it was a blessing that I didn't know the day before that I was going to play or I might not have slept all night. As it was, I was nervous just lobbing the ball back and forth with Gus Triandos, who was playing first base that day.

It was a real thrill though when they made the announcement over the loudspeaker. "Playing third base in place of Leppert, batting sixth, Brooks Robinson."

Eddie Lopat, who was finishing out his career, was our starting pitcher and Chuck Stobbs started for the Senators.

My heart was in my throat when Lopat threw the first pitch of the game to Eddie Yost, the Washington lead-off man. I was concentrating so hard on Yost that I didn't even hear our shortstop, Willie Miranda, yelling at me to play nearer the bag.

Stobbs had no trouble with me the first time I went to bat. I hit an easy grounder to the shortstop and was thrown out by 10 feet.

The second time up, in the fourth inning, I got ahold of one and hit a clean shot over third base for a single. I can remember Mickey Vernon, the Senators first baseman, smiling at me when I came back to the bag after rounding first.

"Nice hit, kid," Vernon said. "Welcome to the big leagues."

I went out the next time up but in the eighth inning I came up with a man on second base. We were ahead 2–1 and I was thinking wouldn't that be something if I could drive in a run in my first major league game and help win it.

Darned if I didn't get a single to drive in the run to put us ahead 3–1. I was really feeling good now, maybe a little cocky.

After the game I went to the phone and called my dad long distance to Little Rock.

"I went two-for-four and got a ribbie, Dad," I told him. "I'm here in the majors to stay. This is my cup of tea. l don't know what I was doing in the minors this year."

I talked too soon. I went 0–for-18 the rest of the season and struck out 10 times. Every time I struck out I thought about what I'd said to my dad.

I learned a good lesson, something I'll never forget.

AL ROSEN

In his first full season (1950), Cleveland Indians third baseman Al Rosen led the American League in home runs with 37, batted .287 and drove in 116 runs. Three years later, he batted .336 with league-leading totals of 43 home runs and 145 runs batted in, and won the Most Valuable Player Award. He holds the unique distinction of adding a Major League Executive of the Year Award to an MVP for his work as general manager of the San Francisco Giants in 1987.

In some respects 1954 was my most memorable year with the Cleveland Indians though from an individual standpoint it wasn't my best season. But that was the season we won 111 games, more than any other American League team ever had won (since surpassed), and if we had won the World Series from the New York Giants it would have been a perfect season.

Everybody knows the story of the '54 World Series, Willie Mays' catch in the Polo Grounds of the ball hit deep to center by Vic Wertz, Dusty Rhodes' hitting, and all the rest. We lost the Series in four games so that was a disappointment, but overall it was a fine season for the Indians and just to get to play in a World Series is a satisfaction denied to many players with longer careers than mine.

An injury I suffered during the '54 season had a lot to do with shortening my career, but it also is part of the story of one of my more memorable days, the All-Star Game that year played in Cleveland.

About a month before the game I fractured my right index finger on a fielding play. It didn't heal as quickly as one might have expected and was still bothering me as the All-Star Game approached.

The game was in Cleveland that year (July 13, 1954), and that was fitting because we were having such a good season as a team. A number of Cleveland players were voted or named to the team, including second baseman Bobby Avila, outfielder Larry Doby, pitcher Bob Lemon and myself.

I wasn't certain I would be able to play, though the fans had voted me to the team. The night before the game I had lain on the finger and it had been so sore I had slept poorly.

The day of the game I wasn't certain what I should do. My finger was bothering me so much that if it had been a normal game I probably would have sat it out.

But in this case I felt I had an obligation to play because the fans had given me more votes than anyone else on the American League team. On the other hand, I went into the game in a bad slump and with my finger the way it was I wasn't sure I could help the team.

Casey Stengel was the manager of the team and I told him my situation before the game. He said he would have to consult Commissioner Ford Frick because the rules said that a player voted to the starting team had to play at least three innings.

It was decided that I would start and take at least one turn at bat, then it would be up to me if I wanted to stay in the game.

My first turn, Robin Roberts, who started for the National League, struck me out and that changed my thinking. Maybe my pride was hurt. I just couldn't bring myself to ask Stengel to take me out. If I had gone out some other way or gotten a hit it might have been different. But to leave after a strikeout—I couldn't bring myself to do it.

Just before I was scheduled to bat in the third inning, I saw Mickey Vernon pick up a bat. Stengel was going to pinch-hit him for me with two men on. I told Casey I wanted to stay in.

Roberts threw me a fastball and I knew it was well hit as soon as I made contact. It cleared the fence in left-center by 15 or 20 feet for a three-run homer.

That picked me up and I didn't think about leaving the game. The next time up, Johnny Antonelli was pitching and he threw me a low curve ball with a man on in the fifth inning. I hit this one even harder and it went some 400 feet into the left field stands.

I was playing first base, though later in the game Stengel switched me to third. I wasn't having trouble in the field either. I was aware of the finger problem but it wasn't bothering me much, not the way I felt.

I got my third hit of the game in the sixth inning, a single off Warren Spahn, and in the eighth Carl Erskine walked me. So, after striking out in my first at-bat, I got on base four straight times, two homers, a single and a walk, and drove in five runs.

The game was a wild one, with six home runs hit, four by the American League, and we won it 11–9. What made it even more outstanding for the Cleveland crowd was that Doby also hit a home run and Avila drove in a couple of runs. Oddly enough, the winning hit was a blooper by Nellie Fox with the bases loaded and the game tied 9–9 in the eighth that drove in two runs.

Another oddity about the game was that the winning pitcher never retired a batter. Stengel brought in Dean Stone with Red Schoendienst on third base in the eighth. Schoendienst made a surprise try to steal home and Stone hurried his motion and threw him out at the plate.

That set off probably the wildest argument of any All-Star Game, the National League arguing that Stone had balked. But the umpires stuck by their call and the inning was over. We rallied for the winning runs in the bottom of the eighth, by which time Stone was gone. He got credit for the win without retiring a single batter.

I can't tell you exactly how I could have had such a fine day with my finger injured the way it was. It was just my day I suppose, which makes it a game I'll never forget. The huge hometown crowd (68,751) undoubtedly gave me a psychological lift and that had a lot to do with it. It got the adrenaline flowing.

Unfortunately, my finger never quite came around. It bothered me from then on and the next two years I couldn't hit up to what I felt was my standard. I was only 32 in 1956 but I decided to retire after that season, though people tried to talk me out of it. When Frank Lane became general manager of the Indians, he urged me to come back after I had sat out a year. He figured the rest should have helped, but I told him I was through playing.

RED SCHOENDIENST

No one was ever associated with the St. Louis Cardinals longer than Red Schoendienst during more than half a century as star second baseman, coach and manager. Schoendienst broke in with the Cardinals in 1945 to begin a 19–year playing career. In his peak year of 1953 he batted .342 with 15 home runs and 79 runs batted in. He managed the Cardinals to two pennants (1967–68). He entered the Hall of Fame in 1989.

I guess you could say it's a coincidence but the two games that have been the most memorable for me were both played in Wrigley Field in Chicago 20 years apart.

No matter what a man says, chances are the first game he ever plays in the big leagues stick out for him right there with any big game he plays later—World Series, All-Star game or pennant-clincher. It's just human nature to feel something extra in your first big league game.

I know I've always felt that way. At least I've always considered the first game I played for the St. Louis Cardinals in April 1945 as one of the high spots of my life.

What I really remember about it isn't anything particularly outstanding. In fact, you might say it was the other way. Sort of embarrassing.

I'd been in the Army in 1944 and when I went to spring training in '45 I wasn't sure what to expect. I'd played just about everything—except pitch and catch—in the minors. The Cardinals didn't have a left fielder that year so I got the job.

We opened the season in Wrigley Field with the Cubs and in the first inning Phil Cavarretta hit a slicing drive to left field. I made a tremendous leap on the ball, got my glove on it, but couldn't hold it. They called it an error.

My first play in the big leagues and it was an error! The official scorer was right. Anytime you get your glove on the ball and don't catch it, it should be an error. But what a way to start! That error on my first chance made it a memorable game for me.

The other game, the one I'll never forget for sure, came twenty years later in the same ballpark. It was my first game as manager of the Cardinals (April 13, 1965), and it just happened that it was in the same park in which I'd played my first major league game.

The weather was typical for Wrigley Field that early in the spring. It was cool, windy and the field was really bad. The groundskeeper said it was the worst he'd seen in more than 30 years after a tough winter.

Everybody was saying before the game that nobody would get any runs, that it figured to be 0–0. After all, we had Bob Gibson starting. He'd won 19 games the year before, then two in the World Series when we beat the New York Yankees. The Cubs started Larry Jackson, who'd won 24 games in 1964.

Those two pitchers and the cold weather made it seem sure nobody'd be doing much hitting. That shows you again you can't count on anything in baseball. Every time the Cubs and Cardinals get together something is sure to happen and this Opening Day it did.

We got five runs in the first inning off Jackson and three of them were a gift. With the bases loaded and two out, Gibson hit a pop fly to the rookie Cubs shortstop, Roberto Pena. The wind caught it and it dribbled off his glove and all three men scored.

I was thinking it was a pretty good way for a rookie manager to start out. But things kept happening. The Cubs got two runs in the second inning and two more in the third when Pena led off with a home run.

That kid had quite a day. He dropped another pop-up by Gibson behind second in the fourth and we scored two more runs to lead 7–4.

Gibson got into trouble again in the Cubs fourth. A couple of men got on and Pena drove them in with a double. We were leading only 7–6 and I made my first pitching change as a manager. I brought in Tracy Stallard, a right-hander.

Stallard had looked good in spring training and he looked even better in this game. He was getting the

Cubs to hit his pitches and we scored runs in the sixth and ninth innings to go into their ninth with a 9–6 lead.

The situation looked good. I was already thinking about my first dinner as a winning big-league manager after Stallard retired the first two Cubs in the bottom of the ninth.

Stallard then walked Ron Santo, only the third man to get on base off him in four and one-third innings, all on walks. He hadn't allowed a hit. I had Barney Schultz warming up just in case.

The next batter, George Altman, singled to left. Two and two out and I figured it was time for Schultz. It wasn't a tough decision at all. Stallard had pitched well but Barney was the big man in the bullpen. He'd been a big reason why we won the World Series in '64.

Schultz had a good spring. He hadn't allowed a run in his last 14 innings of pitching. That was proof enough for me he was ready for the season. I wanted his knuckleball against Ernie Banks, who was the next Cubs hitter.

Schultz got the count up to 2–2 on Banks, then Ernie hit it. I can still see that drive, curving high into the left field bleachers. Three runs across and the game tied 9–9. The game everybody figured nobody would be able to hit in!

We got the next out and had a chance to score in the 10th when Pena made his third error of the game, but didn't do it. Schultz got the side out in the Cubs 10th and got on base in the 11th. Lou Brock scored him with a single and we were ahead 10–9.

We couldn't hold it in the Cubs 11th. Pena led off with a single and scored on a double by Santo to tie the game 10–10. That's the way it ended because the umpires called the game after the last Cubs out.

All Pena did that day was make three errors, get three hits and drive in four runs. He batted .500 and fielded about the same.

That game went four hours and 12 minutes and 11 innings, and after my first day as big league manager was over I still didn't have a won-lost record.

That's something I'll never forget.

Photo by Clifton Boutelle

TOM SEAVER

A five-time 20-game winner who won a total of 311 games during a 20–year career (1967–86), right-hander Tom Seaver was the pitching mainstay of the 1969 "Miracle Mets" so adored by their New York fans. He led the National League three times in victories and five times in strikeouts on his way to the Hall of Fame.

I still get needled about Jimmy Qualls. Even now.
Even after the years that have gone by. People still say,
"Imagine that, Qualls!" They don't let me forget it. But
do I have any regrets? Lord, no! When you pitch a one-
hit shutout in the middle of a pennant race that in itself
is a very memorable game.

That's the one of course, the one-hit game I pitched
against the Chicago Cubs in Shea Stadium in 1969. No
other game sticks out for me quite like that one. How
could it?

You have to remember the situation in July 1969. The
Cubs came into New York on July 8, 1969 five games in
front of us (New York Mets). We were in second place,
but the Cubs weren't taking us seriously as contenders.
Not too many people were.

Just before the first game of the series, Ron Santo, the
Cubs third baseman, made a comparison of their
lineup with ours, pointing out how in almost every
case Chicago had an established star at a position while
we had young, relatively little-known players.

The Cubs did have a good team—Santo, Ernie
Banks, Glenn Beckert, Randy Hundley, Don Kessinger,
Billy Williams—and maybe our guys weren't as well
known.

But Santo totally underrated our ball club. He
underrated our defense, and he wasn't aware of the
kind of pitching we had. We had very strong, very
good pitching. Our pitching was young, none of us—
Jerry Koosman, Gary Gentry, Nolan Ryan, Tug
McGraw and myself—having been around more than
two or three years. I guess maybe there was room for
speculation.

Players will frequently do what Santo did, compare
lineups and overlook the importance of pitching. If
they do that, they're going to be wide open to make a
mistake. You know, pitching is the most significant

factor on any team. Strong pitching can outweigh other major flaws.

I don't have to remind anyone of how important pitching proved for the Mets that season. That's on the record.

We beat the Cubs in the first game of the series on July 8, pulling out the game with three runs in the ninth inning—after going in trailing 3–1. After the game, Santo blasted Don Young, the Cubs center fielder, for not having caught two flyballs that fell for hits in the ninth. Leo Durocher, the Cubs manager, also blasted Young.

The next night, Wednesday, July 9, Qualls was in center field for the Cubs instead of Young. Qualls was a rookie who had been in just a few games and was hitting around .230.

Nobody on our club knew anything about Qualls except Bobby Pfiel, who had played against him in the minors. "He usually gets wood on the ball, and sprays it around," Pfiel told me. "Throw him hard stuff."

There'd never been a crowd like that to see us in Shea Stadium before. There were 60,000 people packed in there that night when I walked out to the mound. My wife Nancy was in the stands and so was my father. He'd come in from the West Coast, and came to the ballpark directly from the airport.

I could feel the tension, the excitement, the expectations of the crowd more than I had ever sensed it before. It was stimulating, but it also put pressure on me. You couldn't help but feel it.

I was a little concerned when I warmed up because my shoulder felt tight. It took a couple of innings before it loosened up, before the adrenaline started to flow and ease up the shoulder.

Ken Holtzman pitched for the Cubs, and we got to him right away. Tommie Agee hit the first pitch for a triple, and Pfiel doubled him in. We were ahead 1–0 after Holtzman had thrown just two pitches.

We scored two more runs in the second inning. I drove in one of them with a double. We got another run in the seventh when Cleon Jones hit a home run to make it 4–0.

Meanwhile, I was retiring the Cubs in order inning after inning. The shoulder that had felt stiff when the game started felt just great. I was throwing harder than I'd ever thrown. I struck out five of the first six Cubs I faced, and when they hit the ball they hit it at somebody.

You try to isolate yourself from the crowd noise during a ball game, to retain your concentration, but as the game continued it got harder and harder to do. By the seventh inning the crowd was cheering every pitch. With every out they were standing up and giving me an ovation.

When Williams went out to end the Cubs seventh he was the 21st batter I had retired in order. I hadn't walked a man. I had a perfect game going. Everybody in the ballpark knew it. Nobody on our bench said a word to me but I knew what was going on. How could I help knowing?

Santo, Banks, Al Spangler. They all went out in the eighth. With every out the crowd roared, 60,000 people yelling, roaring, cheering me, pulling for me to pitch a perfect game. Three outs to go. I felt I could do it.

The hitters in the ninth were Hundley, Qualls, then a pinch hitter for the pitcher. When I went out to the mound I heard a roar greater than the ones before. Everybody was standing up and cheering.

Hundley squared away to bunt. He laid it down, but I got off the mound quickly and threw him out. Two outs to go!

Qualls stepped in, a left-handed hitter. The first time up he'd hit a fast ball to the warning track in right field. The next time he'd hit a curve ball very sharply to first base. I was trying different pitches on him, but he seemed to get a piece of everything.

This time I tried to pitch him away with a fast ball. The ball didn't sink. It stayed up, and Qualls got the bat on it. He hit a line drive to the gap between Tommie Agee in center and Jones in left. It fell for a single.

Disappointed? Of course, at the moment. I'd like to have pitched a perfect game. Anybody would.

But I got the next two batters out, Willie Smith, then Kessinger, and the game was over, a one-hitter. We'd won 4–0.

When I walked from the dugout through the tunnel toward the locker room, I saw Nancy. She had tears in her eyes. "What are you crying for?" I said. "We won 4–0."

I still feel the same way. Regrets? How can you have regrets about a one-hitter you pitched in the middle of a pennant race?

DUKE SNIDER

Chances are Duke Snider could have been elected mayor of Brooklyn during his halcyon days with the Dodgers when he was the star center fielder of one of the greatest teams of all time. Snider hit 407 home runs during his 18–season (1947–64) career, with four consecutive years of 40 or more. He played in six World Series with the Dodgers, the last coming in Los Angeles in 1959. He was inducted into the Hall of Fame in 1980.

There are many games that stick out in my mind, but I think the most interesting thing that ever happened to me was overcoming the insecurity I felt about ever becoming a real major leaguer.

I had a good season with the Brooklyn Dodgers in 1949, my first year as a regular. I hit more than 20 homers, drove in more than 90 runs, and batted .292. On top of that, we won the pennant and went into the World Series against the New York Yankees.

But the '49 Series was a nightmare for me, I was such a failure. Not only did we lose to the Yankees, but I tied Roger Hornsby's record for striking out in a five-game Series. I struck out eight times in five games, which is a bunch. I was such a failure that it raised doubts in my mind about whether I'd really be a success as a big leaguer.

It took three years for me to set those doubts to rest. In '51, of course, we lost the playoffs to the New York Giants when Bobby Thomson hit that home run. Then, in '52,we won the pennant again. Even though we lost the Series to the Yankees, I feel that was the turning point of my career.

For three years, since '49, I'd had a little doubt in my mind whether I was a clutch player or not. But in that '52 Series I hit four homers, which restored my confidence. I hit the ball well against pitchers like Vic Raschi and Allie Reynolds, the same men who'd struck me out so easily in '49. That was the turning point of my career because it gave me the impetus to go on and make the most of the ability I had.

Those were the great years at Brooklyn, the early and mid-'50s.

I can't think of a better team than the one we had, not with players like Roy Campanella, Pee Wee Reese, Jackie Robinson, Carl Furillo, Carl Erskine and the rest.

It was a perfect team for Ebbets Field, which was my favorite park to hit in.

We did well, but there was one hump we could never get over until '55, and that was winning the World Series. Almost every year the Yankees were in our way, and somehow or other they always beat us.

Then came '55, and the game, or the games, I'll never forget. I say games because I didn't do all that much in the final one, the one in which we beat the Yankees to win the Series for the first time. That meant the most to me, just winning the Series, but I've also got to think about the fifth game because I contributed the most to beating the Yankees in that one.

The seventh game is the one in which Johnny Podres pitched the shutout to beat the Yankees 2–0. I didn't do anything spectacular, but I was involved in a play that helped produce our second run of the game in the sixth inning.

Pee Wee singled off Tommy Byrne, pitching for the Yankees, in the sixth inning. I laid down a bunt for a sacrifice to move Pee Wee to second. Moose Skowron, the first baseman, fielded the ball and as I ran down the line I brushed the ball out of his glove to reach first safely.

We got a run out of that because after Campy moved the runners along Furillo walked and Gil Hodges hit a sacrifice fly to score Pee Wee from third.

That was just one of the high spots in that game, the one in which Sandy Amoros in left field made that great catch on Yogi Berra's sinking fly to start a doubleplay and end a Yankee rally. That game brought us our first championship, so in that it was the greatest I've ever been involved in.

I can't overlook the fifth game of the same Series though because it was one of the greatest days of my career from a personal standpoint. It was certainly a game I'll never forget.

The Series was tied 2–2 with the Yankees and we were playing in Brooklyn (October 2, 1955). Bob Grim was the Yankees pitcher and Roger Craig started for us.

We'd lost the first two games of the Series, then won the next two. If I remember right, at that time no team ever had lost the first two games of a Series then come back to win.

I'd hit two homers in the first four games, giving me seven altogether in World Series play. Before I came to the ballpark that day somebody said to me I had a chance of tying Joe DiMaggio's performance of eight home runs in World Series play.

Ever since I was a kid, Joe always had been an inspiration to me as a center fielder and as a hitter. I always considered him to be one of the greatest ballplayers ever to put on a uniform. Even to be mentioned in the same sentence with him was a boost for me.

Strangely, during the season I hadn't hit a homer since Labor Day. All I can say is that I wasn't really shooting for homers after we clinched the pennant, but when the Series came along I realized there was a job to do.

That Yankee pitcher, Grim, had good stuff. He threw me as good a curve as I've ever seen in the third inning. It came inside and I was lucky to get good wood on it. I hit it over the right field screen to boost our lead to 3–0.

My next turn at bat, in the fifth inning, Grim threw me another curve, this one on the outside. I don't think I ever hit a better pitch. I missed one just like it before the homer. This one sailed over the right field screen, just like the first one.

I also got a double in that game, giving me three-for-four, two of them homers.

You can get some idea of how I felt when I hit my second homer of the game and passed DiMag. You bet I knew it, and it went down as one of the greatest thrills of my career. Later, I passed Lou Gehrig, who hit 10 Series homers, and I ended my career with 11.

I won't say that was the happiest day of my career because that didn't come until two days later when we beat the Yankees in the seventh game to win the World Series for Brooklyn for the first time.

But it was a game I'll never forget, and I can't think of a greater thrill from an individual standpoint.

JOE TORRE

Directing the New York Yankees to World Series championships in 1996 and 1998 added further luster to Joe Torre's exceptional career as player, manager and broadcaster. Torre reached his peak in 1971 as the St. Louis Cardinals third baseman when he won the National League Most Valuable Player Award after leading the league in batting with .363 and in runs batted in with 137. In addition to the Yankees, he managed the New York Mets, Atlanta Braves and Cardinals.

It was a dandy, I'll tell you that, and I'll remember it as long as I live because a game like that comes along once in a lifetime—and some people might say that's enough.

The game I'm talking about, the game I'll never forget, is the 25-inning game we played at Shea Stadium in New York in 1974 (September 11) when I was with the St. Louis Cardinals against the New York Mets.

Naturally, when you've been in baseball as long as I have, there are a lot of other games you remember for one reason or another, though I was never fortunate enough to play in a World Series. But there were some All-Star games, in one of which I hit a home run, and other games, like the one in which I hit for the cycle.

But that extra, extra-inning game tops them all. It got to the point where you wondered if it would end and whether you'd get to bed before it was time for breakfast. As it turned out, it was a near thing.

Jerry Koosman was the starting pitcher for the Mets and Bob Forsch for us. Koosman threw the first pitch at a minute or two after eight to Lou Brock, our leadoff hitter and, obviously, nobody had any idea it would be more than seven hours later that the last pitch would be thrown.

We got to Koosman early with a run in the first. He was a little wild and walked Brock and Reggie Smith, and I scored Brock with a single. That was the only run we got until the ninth.

Koosman got himself straightened out, and seemed in control of the game. The Mets got a run in the bottom of the first to tie the game 1–1, then Cleon Jones hit a home run with a man on in the third.

We never really threatened Koosman again until the ninth and that 3–1 lead stood up. I remember getting another hit. I also remember making a couple of diving plays to save hits down the line, though I don't recall who hit the ball.

The ninth inning came around pretty fast and it looked like if we couldn't tie it, it would be a two-hour game. The way Koosman was going, our chances didn't look good. I think we had only three hits going into the ninth.

But in the top of the ninth, Ted Simmons beat out an infield hit, and a couple of outs later Kenny Reitz hit a home run to tie the game 3–3.

I can't remember too many of the details of the next 16 innings. All I know is that we'd get runners on, chances to score, but somehow could never push a run across. The same for the Mets. It just went on and on, the manager changing pitchers, sending in pinch hitters, pinch runners, but nobody could push a run across.

The guy you had to marvel at was the plate umpire, Ed Sudol. He was behind the plate all night. The funny thing about it was that he'd been behind the plate six years earlier when the Mets played a 24-inning game against Houston, and also in another game in 1964 between the Mets and San Francisco that went 23 innings.

He told us about it later, saying, "Why does it always happen with the Mets?"

Another sidelight to the game was that Commissioner Bowie Kuhn had brought his family out that night and, you've got to give him credit, he stuck it out right to the end.

All I remember between the ninth inning and the 25th is an incident in the 20th when I was partly responsible for Mets Manager Yogi Berra being kicked out.

Mets catcher Duffy Dyer got in my way when I bounced one in front of the plate and Sudol called obstruction, awarding me first base. Berra came out to argue and Sudol ejected him.

That really didn't make any difference as far as the game was concerned. Neither club could score, though we both had enough chances. I think we had something like 18 hits and a dozen walks in the game, and the Mets weren't much short of that.

But though each club could get runners on, they couldn't get them across. It wasn't that there was exceptional defense, it's just that extra-inning games have a tendency to be like that.

They just work that way. What happens is that you get to a point where everybody's trying to win the game by themselves. I think that in extra innings you get to a situation in which everybody loses sight of fundamentals. You get to a point where everybody's going to end the thing right now instead of doing the things you do best to try and help win it.

It was around three in the morning—and there weren't all that many left in the crowd that was there seven hours earlier—that we finally scored a run. It wasn't pretty, but it looked beautiful to us.

Bake McBride scratched a hit off Hank Webb, who must have been the sixth Mets pitcher, to lead off the 25th. Webb tried to pick him off, but threw the ball past the first baseman, John Milner, who chased it into right field.

McBride was rounding third base by the time Milner recovered the ball, and he wasn't about to stop. I guess he was determined to end the game. Milner made a good throw to the plate, but the catcher, Ron Hodges, fumbled the ball and McBride scored. It took two errors on the play, and we were ahead 4–3.

So we got the run, and we got the Mets out in the bottom half of the 25th to win 4–3.

When the game ended, it was a little after 3 A.M., and it has lasted seven hours and four minutes, the longest night game in history.

It had been better than a 12-hour day at the park for me. Myself, I'm always at the park for a night game, usually about three o'clock or so. I remember when we finished this one, finished showering and whatever, we went into New York and it was too late to get a beer at the Stage Delicatessen. They stopped serving beer about 4 A.M.

That wasn't the end of it. The next day we played a nine-inning game and it went three hours. We won that game, and then we had to go to Philly. That game at Philly went 17 innings, and we won it by scoring five runs in the 17th.

That 25-inning game, that's the one I'll remember though. That was a dandy.

BILL VEECK

It's doubtful if any team owner has been as flamboyant or inventive as Bill Veeck, the consummate showman who at one time or another controlled the Cleveland Indians, St. Louis Browns and Chicago White Sox. His most memorable gimmick might have been to bring a midget to bat for the St. Louis Browns, but he also gave a legendary African-American pitcher his belated opportunity to compete in the major leagues.

There are two games that are very close in importance to me among the many I saw in my years in baseball, and yet it's not hard to choose between them as to
which was the most important.

One of those games would be the one in which the
Cleveland Indians defeated the Boston Red Sox in the
playoff for the American League pennant in 1948.
That's the one in which Lou Boudreau [the playing-
manager] hit two home runs.

The other one also was a game in 1948, and that
would really have to be the big one in my memory, the
game I'll truly never forget. That's the one Leroy
[Satchel] Paige pitched at Comiskey Park against the
Chicago White Sox after he joined the Indians in 1948.

How could I ever forget that game? According to the
records Satch drew 51,013 fans, the largest crowd ever
to see a night game at Comiskey Park. But in point of
fact there were probably 70,000 people there.

The people just surrounded the park and threatened
to break the gates down. I asked Mrs. Grace Comiskey,
owner of the White Sox, "Why don't you just let them
in before they break the fences down?" It was an
incredible sight. People were coming around the gates,
over them, under them, milling around.

The crowd was so great that they simply burst
through the police lines like a tidal wave, and
swamped the turnstiles. It was impossible for them to
leave even if they had wanted to. And nobody wanted
to, that's for sure.

I didn't even have a seat, it was so crowded. I got
tickets for Sidney Schiff, one of my partners, who came
with a group. It took them three-quarters of an hour to
fight their way from the cab that brought them to the
park from the hotel.

Not having a place to sit, I was pushing my way
through the crowd when I noticed Schiff and his group

crouched against the railings far from the seats they were supposed to have. I asked, "What are you doing here? Why aren't you in your seats?"

Schiff said, "Joe Louis [heavyweight champion] and a group of his friends are in our seats and I'm not about to fight him for them."

It was just an incredible sight, and it was a vindication to me after the furor that had been aroused when I signed Paige. People were accusing me of making a travesty of the game, of creating a cheap publicity stunt by signing Satchel, who was supposed to be between 42 and 55 years of age.

Taylor Spink of *The Sporting News* wrote a ferocious, long editorial in which he ripped me up and down. He was my most vocal opponent. Every time Paige pitched, I'd sent Spink a wire about the results: five hits, seven strikeouts, no runs. Finally, Spink wrote another editorial apologizing to me.

My vindication was complete the first full game Satch pitched for the Indians that night of August 13, 1948 when it seemed as if all Chicago turned out to see what he could do against the White Sox.

He did all that could be expected right from the start. He was in control all the way in that game, with his assortment of fast balls, hesitation pitches and "bat dodgers." He threw overhand and three-quarters, and he kept the Sox popping up He didn't walk a man all night.

All the Sox could get off him were five singles.

Satch always could rise to the occasion like that. For Satch, it was the big ones that counted, and that was a big game for us when you consider we had to go all the way to a playoff for the pennant, and were never ahead by much all season.

So all he did was beat the White Sox 5–0 in a game that was all-important in several respects—for the

Indians, for myself and for him, in that proved he could go nine innings without trouble. It certainly showed our detractors that this wasn't just a cheap publicity stunt, that we got Paige because we thought he could help us win a pennant.

After the game, naturally, I went to the locker room to see Satch.

He gave me that funny little grin he always had after a game.

"I kept 'em from running us both out of town," he said, referring to the fuss that went up when we signed him. He was soaking his arm in hot water, as he always did for an hour after a game, and he added, "Never a doubt, Burrhead." He always called me Burrhead.

Last summer (1971), when I went up to Cooperstown to see him inducted into the Hall of Fame, he again made reference to the fact we were both on the spot in that game in Chicago in 1948. "Never in doubt, Burrhead."

I can still see him, leaning over, looking at the catcher, giving Luke Appling of the White Sox that triple windup, the hesitations, the slow, slow, and slower treatments until Luke was ready to pounce on the ball and beat it to death.

Of course, that was the big one, but he pitched just about like that the rest of the season for us. A week after that game in Comiskey Park he again beat the White Sox, this time 1–0 in Cleveland in a game that drew 78,342, at that time the largest crowd ever to see a night game.

He was a tremendous help to us the last two months of that season. I don't believe we could have won the pennant without him in 1948. He had a 6–1 record, he saved two or three other games, and he came up with the big ones when we needed them.

You wouldn't believe some of the criticism that was directed against us when we signed him in July. A lot of people said I was just trying to hype attendance, and that I could possibly hurt the Indians' chances for a pennant. They charged that as great a pitchers as Satch had been in the Negro leagues, he was washed-up, and it was too late for him to pitch in the majors.

They also said a lot of other things which weren't so nice.

But it all stopped after that game he pitched against the White Sox in Comiskey Park. That was complete vindication for both of us, and it was one of the major steps we took that season in winning the pennant for Cleveland for the first time since 1920.

As Satch said, he kept 'em from running us out of town.

Photo by Ron Mrowiec

CARL YASTRZEMSKI

"Yaz" was a worthy successor to the great Ted Williams as the idol of the Boston Red Sox. He was a fine outfielder, and an exceptional left-handed hitter, who won three American League batting titles. He's one of only a handful of players, including Williams, ever to win the batting Triple Crown. His career of 23 years (1961–83) was one of the longest in major league history.

The game I'll never forget was played on the last day of the 1967 season, the one in which the Red Sox won the pennant to bring to life what they later called "The Impossible Dream."

It has to be the game that day not only because we won the pennant but because it capped my finest year.

Everything seemed to fall into place for me that season, and finishing on top made it perfect. The only disappointment we had was not winning the World Series from the St. Louis Cardinals, but it was an achievement to get into it.

Nobody really figured us to win that year. It was still a 10–club league in 1967, and until July it looked like Chicago, Detroit and Minnesota would fight it out for the pennant that year.

We started coming on in July, though, and people started taking us seriously after we went to Chicago for a weekend series of five games and won three from the White Sox in late August. We were in the middle of things.

We stayed right there through September as first one, then the other of the four clubs going for the pennant put on a surge only to fade back. For a while it looked like the White Sox would win it, but then the last week of the season the Kansas City A's took two from them in one day.

That put Detroit in good position. The Tigers went into the final weekend with four single games against the California Angels at Detroit. If they won all four, they'd have the pennant.

But it rained the first two days in Detroit, and the Tigers were forced to play doubleheaders on Saturday and Sunday, the last two days of the season, which figured to put a strain on their pitching.

Our last two games were against Minnesota, Saturday, September 30, and Sunday, October 1, at Fenway Park in Boston. The Twins were a game ahead of us in first place, with a 91–69 record. The Tigers were a game back with an 89–69 record, and we were 90–70, also a game out.

To win the pennant, we had to beat the Twins twice, and the Angels had to beat the Tigers at least two of the four games they had left.

We won the game from the Twins 6–4 on Saturday to pull into a first-place tie with them while the Tigers were splitting with the Angels at Detroit.

There was something else at stake, too, in that Saturday game. Both Harmon Killebrew of the Twins and I went into the game with 43 home runs. I wanted to beat him out bad because I was leading the league in batting and in runs batted in and if I won the home run title, too, I'd get the Triple Crown.

I had a good day. I had three hits, and drove in four runs, three with my 44th home run, off Jim Merritt, who was the third Twins pitcher. But Killebrew hit a home run, too, so that added even more excitement and pressure—if possible—to the final day of the season.

Everything was on the line for us Sunday. If we beat the Twins, and the Angels could beat the Tigers at least one of their two games in Detroit, the pennant was ours. Even if the Tigers won both their games we could force them into a playoff by winning.

And the home run title was on the line, too, the Triple Crown with it. If Killebrew hit his 45th and I didn't get one, I'd lose the Triple Crown few men ever have won.

I can tell you I didn't get much sleep Saturday night, thinking about what was at stake, and worrying about whether I'd be able to hit Dean Chance, a real good right-hander who was pitching for the Twins Sunday. Chance already had won 20 games.

Manager Dick Williams had saved Jim Lonborg, our top pitcher who already had won 21 games, to throw against the Twins.

The Twins got in front 1–0 in the first inning, which was something to worry about with a guy like Chance pitching. They got another run in the third when, with Cesar Tovar on first, I played a single by Killebrew into an error, permitting Tovar to score.

You can imagine how that made me feel, though I'd gotten a single off Chance my first time up. I felt a little better when I got another single in the third inning. But we didn't score, and we were still behind 2–0 when our turn came in the fifth.

Lonborg beat out a bunt to start it out. Jerry Adair singled and then Dalton Jones got another single to load the bases. I was up, thinking we had Chance on the spot. We couldn't afford to let him off the hook.

I waited for my pitch. I figured Chance would come in with a sinker low and away sooner or later. I let the first pitch, a fast ball inside, go by for ball one. Now I was ready for the sinker. All I had to do was meet the ball, not try to kill it.

I guessed right. He threw the sinker, low and outside. I got the bat on it, and lined the ball over the second baseman's head to drive in Lonborg and Adair with the tying runs.

Before the inning was over, we got three more runs and had a 5–2 lead. We had all the runs we needed. Lonnie gave up another run in the eighth, but hung on.

The moment the game was over, I sprinted for the dugout. The fans were pouring onto the field, and if they'd caught me they'd have torn my uniform to shreds for souvenirs. As it was, I got pawed over and felt lucky to escape alive.

I'd gone four-for-four in the last game, and got six hits in my last six trips to finish the season. Lonnie had kept Killebrew from hitting another home run, and we shared the title with 44. I'd won the Triple Crown with a batting average of .326 and 121 ribbies to go with the 44 homers.

But when the game was over, we still hadn't won the pennant clear. The Tigers beat the Angels in the first game, and the second one was still being played. If they won that one, they'd tie us with a 92–70 record. We didn't want a playoff. You could never tell what might happen.

We all gathered around the radio near my locker listening to the game in Detroit. The Tigers led early but the Angels took a 4–3 lead in the third inning. That brought a big cheer from all the guys.

We still didn't feel too confident. That's a small ballpark in Detroit, and it didn't take much to score a lot of runs. The Tigers could do it. We'd had it happen to us.

The Angels added to their lead, and pretty soon they were ahead 7–3. But the Tigers kept hacking away and it was 8–5 when they came up for their last turn in the ninth.

It was deathly quiet in our locker room when the Tigers got two men on base in the ninth with nobody out. The beer and sandwiches were untouched. But the third batter went out, and when Dick McAuliffe hit into a doubleplay to end the game we went wild.

We tore the place apart, and it was champagne instead of beer. We'd won the pennant.